Philosophies
at
War

Philosophies
at
War

A R C H B I S H O P
FULTON J. SHEEN

TAN Books
Gastonia, North Carolina

Philosophies at War published by TAN Books 2022

Cover & interior design by www.davidferrisdesign.com

Cover image: Intelligence, simplicity, spirituality, humor are all expressed in the features of Bishop Fulton Sheen, once described as a "priestly-looking Tyrone Power". (Photo by Bettmann / Getty Images).

ISBN: 978-1-5051-2331-9

Kindle ISBN: 978-1-5051-2332-6

ePUB ISBN: 978-1-5051-2333-3

Published in the United States by
TAN Books
PO Box 269
Gastonia, NC 28053

www.TANBooks.com

CONTENTS

PUBLISHER'S NOTE

ARCHBISHOP FULTON J. SHEEN (1895–1979) was one of the greatest theologians of the twentieth century. As the first Catholic televangelist on prime-time television, his program, Life is Worth Living, inspired an audience of nearly thirty million people weekly, more listeners than St. Paul ever could have reached during a lifetime of preaching. With his eloquent writing and preaching on television and radio, he movingly and masterfully portrayed life, eternity, love, sorrow, joy, freedom, suffering, marriage, and so much more. His memorable style was distinguished by his booming voice, his Irish wit and wisdom, and his warm smile.

In this carefully selected set of books, Sheen offers clear guidance on the problems affecting all people in today's world, including key ideologies that seek to destroy the Church and society, including Marxism and Freudianism, what is today called "Cultural Marxism." His spiritual and practical wisdom cover a wide variety of subjects that range from discussions of down-to-earth spiritual and moral problems to provocative conversations on the meaning of life, family, education, Christianity, world affairs, and more. Together they add up to a stirring and challenging statement of Bishop Sheen's whole philosophy of life and living. With ease, Sheen shows the relationship between human reason and religion. He shows that the world of today has reached a point of irrationalism that is in utter contempt of lasting truths. With honesty and capable scholarship, Sheen has something to say for everyone. His works are of immediate concern to all men and women seeking understanding, belief, and purpose in these troubled times.

Bishop Sheen reminds us that if we are to help cure the modern world of pessimism and despair, hatred and confusion, we must enlist as warriors of love and peace. Sheen's daily Holy Hour before the Most Blessed Sacrament was the catalyst behind his preaching and writing but also his great love for the Blessed Mother. She was the woman he loved most, "The World's First Love," in addition to his great love for St. Thérèse, patroness of the foreign missions.

Sheen wrote over seventy books, many of which are still widely read today. When the first nationwide Catholic Hour was inaugurated in 1930 on NBC, Sheen was chosen as the first preacher. He hosted this nighttime radio program for twenty years from 1930 to 1950 before moving to television where he had his own show on prime-time TV from 1952 to 1957. Sheen twice won an Emmy for Most Outstanding Television Personality and was featured on the cover of Time magazine. But more important than any earthly awards, Fulton Sheen's tireless evangelization efforts helped convert many to the Faith, especially Communist organizer Bella Dodd.

Entombed in a side altar at the Cathedral of Saint Mary of the Immaculate Conception in Peoria, Illinois, Sheen's cause for canonization was officially opened in 2002. May readers be inspired by Archbishop Fulton J. Sheen, a timeless voice described as one of the greatest Catholic philosophers of our age.

CHAPTER ONE

War and Revolution

There are two ways of looking at the war: one as a journalist, the other as a theologian. The journalist tells you what happens; the theologian not only why it happens, but also what matters. If we look at this war through the eyes of a journalist or a commentator, it will be only a succession of events without any remote causes in the past, or any great purpose in the future. But if we look at the war through the eyes of God, then the war is not meaningless, though we may not presently understand its details. It may very well be a purposeful purging of the world's evil that the world may have a rebirth of freedom under His Holy Law, for:

> Every human path leads on to God,
> He holds a myriad finer threads than gold,
> And strong as holy wishes, drawing us
> With delicate tension upward to Himself.[1]

---

[1] E. C. Stedman, *Protest of Faith.*

Our approach is from the divine point of view, first of all, because it is the only explanation which fits the facts; secondly because the American people who have been confused by catchwords and slogans are seeking an inspiration for a total surrender of their great potentialities for sacrifice, both for God and country.

The great mass of the American people are frankly dissatisfied with the ephemeral and superficial commentaries on what is happening. Being endowed with intelligence, they want to know why it is happening. We all know what we are fighting against; we want to know what we are fighting for. We all know that we are in a war; we want to know what we must do to make a lasting peace. We know whom we hate; but we want to know what we ought to love. We know we are fighting against a barbarism that is intrinsically wicked; we want to know what we have to do to make the resurrection of that wickedness impossible.

It is necessary to clear away three false conceptions of the war by reminding ourselves what this war is not.

This war is not merely a political and an economic struggle, but rather a theological one. It is not political and economic, because politics and economics are concerned only with the means of living. And it is not just the means of living that have gone wrong, but the ends of living. Never before in the history of the world have there been so many abundant means of life. Never before was there so much power, and never before have men so prepared to use that power for the destruction of human life. Never before was there so much material wealth; never before has there been so many means to draw people together through rapid communications and the radio; never before have they been so pulled apart by hate and strife and war.

The means of life no longer minister to peace and order because we have perverted and forgotten the true ends of life. Dynamite can be used as a means to build the foundations of a hospital, or it can be used as a means to destroy the entire hospital. The purpose or the intention for which it is used will determine how the means are used. Now the basic reason why our economics and politics have failed as a means to peace is that both have forgotten the end and purpose of life. We have been living as if civilization, culture and peace were by-products of economic activity, instead of the other way round, so that economics and politics are subordinated to the moral and the spiritual. Politics and economics alone are as incapable of curing our ills as an alcohol rub is incapable of curing cancer; and if we assume they will, then this world war will end in socialism, and socialism is only an obligatory and enforced organization of the means of living to prevent utter ruin. It is not our politics that has soured, nor our economics that have rusted; it is our hearts. We live and act as if God had never made us. That is why this war is not political and economic in its fundamental aspects; it is theological.

This war has not been caused by evil dictators. It is too commonly assumed that our milk of international peace has curdled, because a few wicked dictators poured vinegar into it. Hence if we could rid the world of these evil men, we would return to a world of comparative prosperity where we would have to worry only occasionally about a fellow citizen watering our milk. What a delusion! These dictators are not the creators of the world's evil; they are its creatures; they are only boils on the surface of the world's skin; they come to the surface because there is bad blood beneath. It will do no good to puncture the boils, if we leave the source of the infection. Have we forgotten that from 1914–1918 our cry was "rid the world of the Kaiser and we will have peace." Well, we got rid of the Kaiser but we had no peace. On the contrary we prepared for another war in the space of twenty-one years. Now we are shouting, "rid the world of Hitler and we will have peace." We will not! We must rid the world of Hitler, but we will not have peace unless we supply the moral and spiritual forces, the lack of which produced Hitler. There are a thousand Hitlers hidden under the barbarism of the present day. It is indeed significant that the era between 1918 and 1939 was called only an "Armistice" and such it was, an interlude between wars. Peace does not follow the extermination of dictators, because dictators are only the effects of wrong philosophies of life; they are not the causes. They come into environments already prepared for them, like certain forms of fungi come into wet wood. Nazism is the disease of culture in its most virulent form, and could not have come to power in Germany, unless the rest of the world were already sick. Were we honest we would admit that we are all citizens of an apostate world, a world that has abandoned God. For this apostasy, we are all in part responsible, but no more than we Christians who were meant to be the salt of the earth to prevent its corruption. No! It is not the bad dictators who made the world bad; it is bad thinking. It is, therefore, in the realm of ideas that we will have to restore the world!

This war is not like any other war. When hostilities cease, we will not go back again to our former way of life. This war is not an interruption of the normal; it is rather the disintegration of the abnormal. We are definitely at the end of an era of history. The old wells have run dry; the staff of unlimited progress on which we leaned, has pierced our hands; the quicksands of our belief in the unqualified goodness of human nature have swallowed the superstructure of our materialistic world. We are now face to face with a fact which some reactionaries still ignore, namely, that society can become inhuman while preserving all the technical and material advantages of a so-called advanced civilization. We will not get back again to the same kind of a world we had before this war, and he who would want to do so, would want the kind of world that produced Hitler. The world is pulling up its tents; humanity is on the march. The old world is dead!

That brings us to what the war is. There are really two great events in the modern world: the war and the revolution.

A war involves nations, alliances, men, armies, defense plants, guns and tanks. A revolution involves ideas. A war moves on a horizontal plane of land, territory and men; a revolution moves on the vertical plane of ideology, doctrine, dogmas, creeds and philosophies of life. This distinction is very important, for it explains how nations can be on the same side of a war and on different sides of a revolution. Russia, for example, is on our side of the war, but Russia is not yet on our side of the revolution; please God some day it may be. The distinction also explains the war between Germany and Russia. Their conflict is not one of ideologies, for Communism and Nazism are both destructive of human freedom. As President Roosevelt said on February 10, 1940: "The Soviet Union, as a matter of practical fact known to you and to all the world, is a dictatorship as absolute as any other dictatorship in the world."

The war is only an episode in the revolution—something incidental. It is the military phase by which the revolution is working itself out. The revolution is far more important and will long outlast the war, for this world war is not a conflict of nations, as was the last world war, but a conflict of ideologies. It is not so much a struggle between alliances of men, as it is between dogmas and creeds. The battles fought on land and sea and in the air are merely episodes of a greater struggle, which is being waged in the realm of ideas. A far more important question than "Who will win the war?" is the question: "Who will win the revolution?" In other words, what kind of ideologies or philosophies of life will dominate the world, when this war is finished?

A revolution we said involved ideologies, dogmas and creeds. How many philosophies of life are involved in this revolution? It is quite generally and falsely assumed that there are only two: Democracy and the Totalitarianism, or the Christian and the anti-Christian. Would to God it were that simple! There are actually three great philosophies of life or ideologies involved:

First, the Totalitarian which is anti-Christian, anti-Semitic, and anti-human.

Secondly, the Secularist world view which is humanistic and democratic, but which attempts to preserve these values on a non-religious and non-moral foundation by identifying morality with self-interest instead of morality with the will of God.

Thirdly, the Christian world view which grounds the human and the democratic values of the Western World on a moral and religious basis. This Christian view includes not only Christians but also Jews, who historically are the roots of the Christian tradition, and who religiously are one with the Christian in the adoration of God and the acceptance of the moral law as the reflection of the Eternal Reason of God.

In the light of these three conflicting philosophies of life our task is three-fold.

This anti-Christian, anti-Jewish and anti-human Totalitarian system must be defeated and crushed not just
because it is a political or economic system contrary to
ours, but because it is anti-human, and it is anti-human
because it is anti-God. Hence our war against it is not in
the name of democracy, but in the name of humanity.

We must fearlessly admit that we are not fighting the
war to keep everything just as it is, for the materialism, selfishness and godlessness which would eat away the vitals
of American traditions, justice and equality we can and
should scrap. Then, having recovered our allegiance to
God's moral law, we may be worthy of our mission to lead
the world to the peace born of the justice and charity of
God, for "Unless the Lord build the house, they labour in
vain that build it. Unless the Lord keep the city, he watch-
eth in vain that keepeth it."

This war is incidental to the great decision the world
must make: whether man is a tool of the state as Totalitarianism believes; or whether man is an animal as the
secularist tradition of the Western World and too many
Americans believe; or whether man is a creature made to
the image and likeness of God as the Christian believes.

There is the essence of conflict.

We have a double enemy in this war, not a single one.
We must defeat the active barbarism from without, and we
must defeat the passive barbarism from within. We must
use our swords with an outward thrust against Totalitarianism and its hard barbarism; but we must also use the sword
with an inward thrust to cut away our own soft barbarism.

In personal language, each of us must say: I must fight
the enemy of man, and I must fight myself when I am my
own worst enemy. We have a war to win; and we have a
revolution to win. A war to win by overthrowing the power

of the enemy in battles and a peace to win by making ourselves worthy to dictate it.

Victory on the field will conquer the hard barbarism.
Repentance and catharsis of spirit alone will conquer
the soft barbarism. Guns, ships, planes, dynamite, facto-
ries, ships and bombs will put down the first evil. Prayer,
sorrow, contrition, purging of our hearts and souls, medi-
tation, reparation, sacrifice and a return to God will alone
accomplish the second. If we merely defeat the hard barbarism and lose to the soft, we will be at the beginning
of cyclic wars, which will return and return until we are
beaten and purged and broken in the creative despair of
getting back to God.

This is the true revolution. All the other revolutions
of the twentieth century have been from without; this
time we want a revolution from within. The revolutions
which shook Europe during the last twenty-five years only
shifted power from one class to another, and booty from
one pocket to another, and authority from one party to
another. This time we want a revolution that will change
hearts! A revolution like the one pictured in "The Magnifi-
cat" which was a thousand times more revolutionary than
the Manifesto of Karl Marx in 1848. The trouble with all
political and economic revolutions is they are not revolutionary enough! They still leave hate in the heart of man!

CHAPTER TWO

The Thing We Are Fighting Against

Of these dogmas or philosophies of life struggling for mastery in this war, we here discuss the first, the anti-Christian totalitarian world view.

This anti-Christian, anti-human, anti-democratic totalitarian ideology exists in four forms widely scattered throughout the world:

In a historical form, as the revival of the imperial traditions of the ancient Roman Empire, which is Fascism.

In an anthropological form, as the glorification of the Nordic race, which is Nazism.

In a theological form, as the identification of Divinity with a dynastic house, which is Japanese Imperialism.

In an economic form, as the proclamation of class struggle on the anti-religious basis of dictatorship of the proletariat, which is Marxian Socialism.

In the Christmas (1942) Encyclical, the Pope condemned these four forms as a "conception which claims for particular nations, or races or classes 'the norm from which there is no appeal.'"

Not one of these four forms is a state in the political sense of the term; rather each is a philosophy of life working through a unique party which acts as a substitute for the State. All agree in investing primitive ideas of class, race, nation and blood with a Divine significance.

Furthermore, as the very word "totalitarian" implies, these systems demand power over the total man—the whole man, body and soul, and aim at control over the most intimate regions of the spirit. In this sense they are religions; only secondarily, are they systems of politics. Because they are religions they persecute Jews and Christians, for in their eyes these are rival religions. In fact, they claim more than Christianity, for Christianity left to Cæsar the things that were Cæsar's, but these new false religions insist that even the things of God belong to Cæsar.

How did these pseudo-mysticisms originate? In their European form they arose in part as a reaction against the excesses and defects of the secularist and materialist culture of the rest of the Western World, just as a man might foolishly burn his barn to get rid of a few rats. Anyone who looks at history in the perspective of the last few hundred years, will see in it a progressive repudiation of Christian principles in social, political and economic life, which repudiation produced first our present non-religious civilization; then an anti-religious civilization (Communism) and finally by reaction the anti-religious one of Nazism against which we are struggling.

Once upon a time there was a Christian culture. It was not a perfect culture, because Christianity was never meant to be perfected in this world. It flowered during the Middle Ages. Chesterton once said that these are called the "Dark Ages" by those who are in the dark about them. The basis of its civilization was that law, education, politics, economics, social service, arts, crafts, labor and capital were all built up in a hierarchical fashion like a pyramid, with God at the peak. Everyone, whether he was a scholar or peasant, lord or serf, sinner or saint, recognized the Lord as the One to Whom he would one day return to render an account of his stewardship. Thus all life was impregnated with morality; economics and politics were branches of ethics; men were one because there was one Lord, one Faith, one Baptism.

This great civilization went into decline partly through the rebirth of pagan ideas and partly through the moral decline of the individuals. There then began what might be called the Era of Substitutions in which men sought other bases for moral unity than the Church. Among these substitutes were the Bible, Reason, and Individual self-interest. Our present non-religious secularist culture grows from these roots.

The first substitute, the Bible, had the great advantage of still keeping society together on the basis of the super-natural and the moral inspiration of Christ the Son of God. But it was unable to maintain that unity long, first of all, because, when every man became an infallible interpreter of the Book, there were as many religions as heads; and because once the Book was detached from the Board of Editors which guaranteed its inspiration, and from a Supreme Court which interpreted it, it became rather the basis of discord than of harmony.

Men then set about for a new bond of cohesion and they sought it in reason—not reason illumined by faith, but reason divorced from faith. The so-called "Age of Reason" was really an Age of Unbelief for its strongest protagonists were corrosive men like Hume, Kant, Voltaire, who measured the growth of reason by its alienation from God Who Alone could guarantee its deliverances and its conclusions. The sovereignty of reasonable people replaced the sovereignty of God. All principles were rejected except a few self-evident ones which, it was hoped, would preserve the brotherhood of man without the Fatherhood of God.

But reason could not hold society together for everyone soon became his own interpreter of reason, as everyone once before was his own interpreter of the Book. As Dean Swift so well described it: "Wisdom is a hen whose cackling we must value and consider because it is attended with an egg. But then lastly it is a nut, which, unless you choose with judgment, may cost you a tooth, and pay you with nothing but a worm."

Finally there came the last and final substitute: the enthronement of individual self-interest, which is known as Liberalism. Men once said, we will not have the Church of Christ rule over us, and then later on added, we will not have the World of God rule over us, then, we shall rule ourselves by our own reason; now they finally decided to rule themselves on the basis of their absolute independence of God.

The three most important principles of this Liberal culture were:

Economically: leave every man free to work out his economic destiny as he sees fit, and the general good of all will result. Upon this non-moral principle modern Capitalism is grounded.

Politically: in order that the individual may be free from restraint in his economic exploitation, the State must have only a negative function like a policeman whose business it is to prevent others from meddling in our affairs, and particularly to preserve property rights.

Socially: Freedom means the right to do whatever you please. A man is therefore most free when he is devoid of all restraints, discipline and authority. Personality is self-expressive when it is unhampered by law.

The Era of Substitution has behind it three great revolutions: the religious revolution which uprooted man from responsibility to a spiritual community; the French Revolution which isolated man from responsibility to a political community or the State; and the Industrial Revolution and Liberalism which isolated man from all responsibility to the social community or the common good. Such is the essence of our secularist culture: the supremacy of the individual man. Torn away from his roots in God, his roots in law and his roots in a brotherhood of men, it naturally led to the anarchy of the jungle and the oppression of the weak and the unfortunate, and a society which was nothing but a criss-cross of individual egotism, where each man was a wolf to his neighbor. And when these egotisms became nationalized and militarized they came to a head in the first World War. Thus did a secularist age, which began with the dream of a universal brotherhood without God, end in a series of frustrated strifes in which men of different races and nations were tempted to deny the last vestige of humanity.

But we failed to learn our lesson after the first World War. We were very much like man after the Flood. Immediately after the deluge, man built for himself the Tower of Babel, by which he affirmed that through his own power and without God's help, he could climb to the heavens. So too after the first World War, which was a deluge, not of water but of blood, man still continued to affirm that by his own power he could build a new world without duties to God and His moral law. One of the Babels produced by human pride was the League of Nations which sought to build a world society not on the moral law, but on balance of power. Nothing better reveals its inadequacy than the fact that in nineteen years of its existence, 4,568 treaties of peace were signed before it; and the year before this war broke out, 211 treaties of peace were signed. These were enough to last until the crack of doom, if nations really believed in what they signed! Nations entered into international agreements in the same spirit a modern man marries—*viz.*: prepared to get a divorce on the grounds of incompatibility when something more attractive comes along.

But something unusual happened after the first World War among certain nations of the world, namely, a reaction against individualism and all its works and pomps.

In three countries revolution broke loose; the revolutions of Nazism, Fascism and Communism. These revolutions were not simply imposed upon the people by cruel dictators. The masses are not stupid; the leaders could never rise to power unless the masses felt that the revolutions were correcting some dreadful abuses.

In every revolution there are two elements: protest and reform. The protests of these revolutionists were right; the reforms were wrong. The appeal of the revolution consisted in its protest against the errors of our secularist culture with its glorification of the individual. Lenin went before the world and said: "Can you not see that an economic system which allows every man to do what he pleases, means that the strong shall be pleased and the weak shall be crushed? Such so-called economic freedom will mean in the end the concentration of wealth in the hands of the few and the impoverishment of the masses. There must be a re-ordering of economic life so that all the economic resources of a nation are bent to the good of all." And in saying this Lenin was right! But though his protest was right, his reform was wrong, for he went to the other extreme and substituted privilege of power for privilege of money, and cured the abuse of property rights by the destruction of all rights.

Mussolini went before his masses and argued: "Can you not see that any political system which asserts that the individual must be kept free from all State control, and which makes the State a policeman, means in the end that the State leaves the weak unprotected against the strong? The State must protect the weak against the strong." In saying this Mussolini was right! But like all reformers he went too far. He got rid of the policeman-State by making the State a nurse and thus extinguished individual freedom and democracy altogether. Such is the error of Fascism: The State is all!

Hitler in his turn argued: "Can you not see that if you define freedom as the right to do whatever you please you will end in anarchy? There must therefore be a restoration of law and authority." And in saying this Hitler was right! But he went too far, as reformers do, and restored law at the expense of freedom. Freedom, which under Liberalism meant the right to do whatever you please, now became freedom to do whatever you must instead of being what we must make it after this war, the freedom to do whatever you ought. Thus did slavery return to the world.

The strength of these totalitarian systems was that they supplied some kind of an answer—false though it was—to the hidden dominance of the lords of finance, to the indifference of democracies to absolute values, and to their claim that the body politic must have precedence over private gain. In the end, however, none of these solutions achieved their goals because none of them understood the nature of man as a creature, endowed with rights because possessing a soul and saddled with duties made by God.

The ills they attempted to cure were basically due to the de-Christianization of society. But through a false diagnosis, they attempted to arrest de-Christianization by anti-Christianizing the world. Because Capitalism, indifference and financial oligarchy sprang up in a civilization whose roots were Christian, they made the mistake of thinking that these evils were due to Christianity. Hence they said: "Religion is the opium of the people." What they failed to see was that, on the field of Western Civilization where grew the wheat of Christianity, some enemies came by night and sowed weeds and thistles. The solution of the problem was not in uprooting the wheat of Christianity but in burning the weeds of our indifference to it.

The story of the last few hundred years is the story of the Prodigal Son. Western Civilization left the Father's House with some of the spiritual substance it had preserved during 1600 years of martyrdom and hard thinking. We are now far enough away from those days to see that it has spent all the capital which it had: the belief in the Divinity of Christ, the inspiration of Sacred Scriptures, the Moral Law and the existence of God. Finally it reached the stage where, like the Prodigal, it fed on husks as a substitute for the bread of the Father's House—the husks of Liberalism, Materialism, Agnosticism.

The Prodigal was right in being hungry; that is the way God made him. The totalitarian States were right in being hungry for Law, the Common Good, and Authority. They were wrong in eating the husks of Fascism, Nazism and Totalitarianism. The right way to look on totalitarian systems is as so many convulsive attempts to arrest the disintegration of society, as the awakening of the conscience of the world against an acquisitive society founded on the primacy of profit, and as a final reminder that man cannot be godless.

Because the enemy is demonic in his philosophy of life, it might be well to recall the words of Our Lord as to how he can be defeated. The disciples on one occasion tried to cast the devil out of a boy possessed. Our Divine Lord did so immediately. The disciples came to Jesus privately and said: "Why could not we cast him out?" He said: "Because of your unbelief. . . . This kind is not cast out but by prayer and fasting" (Matt. 17: 18–20). This service they have done us did we but have the eyes to see. They have the great value of reminding us that unless we get back again to God and His Moral Law, we shall revert to barbarism.

Now that we have suggested the nature of Totalitarianism's origin, as a reaction to fundamental defects in our civilization and as false attempts to arrest its disintegration, we now consider its doctrines.

Totalitarianism has three negative dogmas: it denies the value of a person by affirming the primacy of the mass, the race, the class. It denies the equality of man, and it affirms that evil is the method and the goal of the revolution.

The basic principle of democracy is the sacredness of the individual as a creature endowed by God with inalienable rights. The basic principle of Nazism and other totalitarian systems is that the individual has no rights except those given him by the Party or the State. In America, freedom resides in man; in Nazism, freedom resides in the race. In America, man endows the State with rights which he received from God; in Nazism, the State endows man with rights which it got from Hitler. One of the best expressions of this totalitarian idea—that the individual has no value because all value resides in collectivity—is to be found in that influential German, Karl Marx, who in 1843 rejected the democratic conception of man saying: "That each man has a value as a sovereign being is an illusion, a dream and a postulate of Christianity which affirms that every man has a soul."[1]

Later writing in the first edition of *Das Kapital* he further developed the idea, "If I speak of individuals, it is only in so far as they are personifications of economic categories and representatives of special class relations and interests."

In plain language, this means that Marx had no use for the individual worker or proletariat as such. The person in himself has no value; he has value only as a representative of a revolutionary class. Once the person ceased to be a member of that class, he ceased to have value. This despisal of the human person, as such, is the first dogma of all totalitarian systems. It explains why the individual Jew has no value or rights in Nazism, because he is not a member of the revolutionary race; it explains Fascism which affirms: "society is the end, individuals only the means and the instruments of social ends." It explains the wanton disregard of individual life by the Japanese Imperial Government and the statement of the Japanese educators: "The individual is not an entity but depends upon the whole arising from and kept in being by the State." These low and unspiritual views of man are the beginning of slavery.

Persons lose their identity in Totalitarianism very much like grapes in a wine press; they continue to exist only in the wine. As Hitler wrote in *Mein Kampf:* "There is only one sacred right, and this right is that the blood is preserved pure." Such is the basis of the cruelty of the Nazis to those who are not of their blood, *e.g.*, the Poles. "If," said Hitler,

---

[1] Marx-Engels, *Historical Critical Edition*, Vol 1, p. 590 (Moscow.)

"I am willing to spend the flower of three million of the German race in war, why should I care about extinguishing the scum of seventeen million Poles?" And if Europe today is in chains, it is not because Nazism is cruel in war; it is because Nazism is wicked in principle; it denies the value of man! Against this absorption of man by the State, the present Holy Father said: "The State may demand the goods of its citizens and if need be its blood, but the soul redeemed by Christ—never!"

Next, Totalitarianism denies the equality of man:

American Democracy is founded on the principle of the essential spiritual equality of all men. When President Roosevelt was asked at the end of October, 1942, to whom his four freedoms were meant to apply, he answered: "To everyone, all over the world." This is in keeping with that great Christian message St. Paul delivered to the proud Athenians on the hill of the Areopagus: "God, who made the world and all things therein . . . And hath made of one, all mankind, to dwell upon the whole face of the earth. . . ." For in Him we live and move and have our being, as indeed some of our poets have said: "For we also are His offspring" (Acts 17: 25–28).

Totalitarianism, on the contrary, denies the basic equality of all men as children of God. Men are equal only on condition that they belong to a certain class, a certain race, a certain dynasty, a certain nation. Hitler, therefore, proclaims the superiority of the German race over all the peoples of the earth with the possible exception of the Japanese, for Hitler has discovered that one of the Japanese sun-gods is a first cousin of the German god Wotan.

The persecution of the Jews therefore is not because, as he first claimed, they were too wealthy but simply because they were not Nordic. "As for the Jews," he writes in one of his early decrees, "they have simply been placed out-side the law" as if any signing of a law could make a man a monkey. Once their equality was denied, their properties were dispossessed. "As a foundation for a new currency, the property of those who are not Jews and not of our blood must do service." According to the same principle a Prot-estant Pastor Niemoeller and the Catholic bishops and priests, such as Bishop von Galen of Münster, are denied equality because they put loyalty to Christ above loyalty to the Füehrer.

This silly idea of the superiority of the German race with its anti-Semitism and its anti-Christianity, has had a long history in Prussia in such men as Fichte, Herder, and Treitzscke. It was no mere accident that when Hitler came into power, one of his first official acts was the ordering of the singing of *Die Meistersinger* of Wagner in the Opera of Berlin. The reason for this choice was because that opera glorified Hans Sachs, the poet of Racism and, in tribute to him, Hitler ordered that all the Party Congresses of the Nazis should be held in the city of the birthplace of Sachs. For that reason they have all been held in Nuremburg.

Neither was it an accident that he called the forts erected opposite the Maginot line after Siegfried, the Nor-dic hero whom Wagner popularized in his opera, and to whom Hitler compared the German people. It will be re-called that Siegfried, thanks to a bath in dragon's blood, was made invulnerable except on his back, where an oak leaf had attached itself. Appealing to this myth, Hitler declared that the superior German race could never be de-feated; it could only be betrayed like Siegfried, by a stab in the back.

Neither was it an accident that in his attachment to Richard Wagner, who accustomed three generations of

Germans to the myths of the Nordic and pagan past of Germany, Hitler should have built his nest at Berchtesgaden. For, in his prose works, Wagner wrote that Germany has already had one reincarnation of Siegfried in Frederick Barbarossa who established the first Reich (Bismarck's being called the second). Wagner said that a day would come when this Siegfried-Barbarossa would have a third reincarnation, a "hero who turns against the ruin of his race" . . . the hero wondrously Divine, and when he comes he will make his home over the spot where the bones of Barbarossa and Siegfried now are supposed to lie buried—in Berchtesgaden—where Hitler has his home.[2]

This barbaric racism, which denies the equality of all men, is less a science or even a philosophy than it is a religion—an anti-Christian mysticism which adores a tribal blood as sacred; a narcissistic self-worship with a supreme diabolical conceit, which in the language of Alfred Rosenberg "represents the mystery which has overcome and replaced the old Sacraments of the Church."

Totalitarianism is wicked because it makes evil the method and the goal of the Revolution.

The inspiration for this idea is due principally to Frederick Wilhelm Nietzsche who gave what might be called the moral code of Nazism, understanding moral here as immoral. Nazism is not negative like Communism. Communism is anti-religious; Nazism is not; it is very religious except that its religion is diabolical. There is only one word to describe how it grafted violence on to legality and that is in the phrase of Rauschning: "The Revolution of Nihilism." And such it is! The following of blind irrational myths; the complete turning upside down of traditional morality;

---

[2] Peter Viereck, *Metapolitics*, p. iii (1941).

the enthronement of the will to power. It is almost pointless for us to argue against the Nazis on the ground that they are cruel and unjust, or because they have built their system on another basis than that of justice and righteousness. We are not talking about the same things. What justice is to us, that injustice is to the Nazis.

The inspiration for this idea is due principally to Nietzsche who sought to found a basis for morality other than that of Christianity, which he called slave-morality, and by so doing to release the pent up energies of the will to power. "Morality must be shot at," as he put it. Then adding, "We are probably the first who understand what a pagan faith is . . . the valuing of all higher existence as immoral existence. . . ."

From this principle he gives what he calls a new table: "Become hard" . . . "Man must be trained for war and woman for the relaxation of the warrior; all else is folly. You should love peace as a means to a new war; and the short peace more than the long. I do not exhort you to work, but to fight. Ye say that a good cause will sanctify war! I tell you, it is a good war that sanctifies every cause . . . My code is the code of Dionysius; sensuality and cruelty. There is the struggle: Dionysius or Christ."

Add these three ideas together: the denial of the value of the person which the German Marx proclaimed; the denial of the equality of all men which the German philosophers proclaimed and which Wagner set to music; and the primacy of irrational power, lust and cruelty which the German Nietzsche affirmed, and you have the thing we are fighting against. It is not a nation; it is not a state; it is a spirit, the spirit of anti-Christ, the last and awful perversion of a community that turned its back on God and to whom Satan showed his face.

Let no one stultify himself by believing that Totalitarianism, as we have defined it, in any of its forms can
be Christianized or democratized or humanized; for here
we are dealing not only with wicked men who could be
converted through God's grace but also with a wicked ideology that makes conversion impossible. Erring sheep can
be brought into the sheepfold of Christ, but evil philosophies
which are like wolves cannot. By their very nature they are
anti-Christian because they exalt the herd recognized by the
State, over the person whose value comes from God. That
is why Totalitarianism persecutes the Church. Persecution
could be avoided only by emptying Christianity of Christ,
man of his soul and the soul of its Justice and Charity.

The evil ideology we are fighting today is in revolt
against both humanity and Christianity. Over a century
ago, a German Jew, Heine, by name, warned the world of
how terrible Germany would be gathering up the full fruits
of its Kant and Fichte, how it would revive the spirit of the
ancient Germans "which does not fight in order to destroy
or conquer but simply for the sake of fighting. Christianity—and this is its fairest merit—has in some degree
subdued that brutal Germanic joy of battle, but it could
not destroy it; and when the cross, that restraining talisman, falls to pieces, then will break forth again the ferocity
of the old combatants, the insane berserker rage whereof
northern poets have said and sung. The talisman is rotten,
and the day will come when it will pitifully crumble to dust.
The old stone gods will then arise from the forgotten ruins
and wipe from their eyes the dust of a thousand years, and
at last Thor with his giant hammer will leap aloft and he
will shatter the gothic cathedrals.

"When you hear the trampling of feet and the clash-
ing of arms, ye neighbours children, ye French, be on your

guard . . . Smile not at my counsel, at the counsel of a
dreamer, who warns you against Kantians, Fichteans and
philosophers of Nature. Smile not at the phantasy of one
who anticipates in the realm of reality the same revolution
that has taken place in the region of intellect. The thought
precedes the deed as the lightning the thunder. German
thunder is of true German character; it is not very nimble,
and it rumbles along slowly. But come it will, and when
you hear a crashing such as never before has been heard in
the world's history then know at last the German thunder-
bolt has fallen. At this commotion the eagles will drop dead
from the skies and the lions in the farthest wastes of Africa
will bite their tails and creep into their royal lairs. There
will be played in Germany a drama compared with which
the French Revolution will seem but an innocent idyll. At
present it is true everything is tolerably quiet and, though
here and there someone creates a little stir, do not imagine
that these are the real actors in the piece. They are only the
little curs running about in the empty arena and barking
and biting at each other until the hour comes in which the
troop of gladiators arrives to fight for life and death."

The war is exploding the fallacy that it makes no difference what you believe. It does make a tremendous difference
what we believe, for we act on our beliefs. If our beliefs are
right, our deeds will be right. The evil of the Nazis is that
they practice what they preach. If twenty years ago we had
educated ourselves along the line of Christian morality to
see the utter moral evil and logical absurdity of these ideas,
we would not now have to sacrifice our lives to blot them
from the earth. What we were once tolerant to as a wicked
idea, we must now be intolerant to as a deed.

We were indifferent to good and evil; we ignored
what happened to the soul of man, to his thinking and his

purposes. These states then came on the scene to say that his soul, his thinking and his purposes must be under the domination of the State.

These demonic forces replaced the spiritual anarchy of bourgeois civilization with a semblance of order; they found substitutes for the doubt, the scepticism and sophistication of an irresponsible intelligentsia in the certitude of an absolute authority embodied in a social philosophy. They proved that any world view is better than no world view; and that a regime that possesses some authority is better than a system of no authority. And in doing so, they thrust the issue before us very clearly; it makes a war of a difference what you believe. This conflict is not between men and nations; it is not only a war—it is a revolution!

What has the Western World to offset this evil? Presently it is depending on what Professor Sorokin has called a "Sensate Culture": a pragmatic, liberal and humanistic philosophy of life which affirms the Doctrine of the Sovereign Ego as the ultimate ground of certainty. Such a philosophy is in reality a staff that will pierce our hands. To that point we now move forward.

CHAPTER THREE

Barnacles on the Ship of Democracy

The second world view locked in this world conflict is the non-Christian or secularist view of Western civilization. By secularist ideology, we mean the attempt to preserve human and democratic values on a non-moral and non-religious foundation. Secularism means the separation of the parts of life,—for example, education, politics and economics and family,—from their center, which is God. Each department of life is considered as having absolute autonomy and in no way can be brought under the sway of ethical principles or the sovereign Law of God. Secularism reaches its peak when men say, "business is business," and "religion is religion," as if the way a man worked or the pay he gave to workers had nothing to do with conscience and the moral fibre of a nation. Secularism affirms an absolute irrelevance of the moral to the secular, denies a religious culture, and, if there were one, denies it could be superior to an anti-religious culture. It was the secularist culture St. Paul condemned when he declared the Romans to be guilty in the sight of God: "They are inexcusable. Because that, when they knew God, they have not glorified him as God or given thanks: but became vain in their thoughts. And their foolish heart was darkened" (Rom. 1: 21). Every form of modern secularism implies self-glorification as St. Paul here described it. Rationalism, for example, glorifies human reason by detaching it from the Eternal Reason of God. Political Positivism of modern law glorifies the State as the source of law.

At first it may seem unfair to characterize our present Western civilization as secular. It may be objected that there are millions of Jews, Protestants and Catholics who are leading lives in close union with God. This, of course, is true. But here we are speaking not of a multitude, but of a spirit; not of numbers, but of influences; not of a minority, but of a temper. There is no doubt that a doctor could find some very healthy organs in an incurably cancerous patient, but "cancerous" and not "healthy" would be the accurate description of such a patient. So with the secularist tradition of Western civilization: strong religious lives exist in it, but they are like a Church in a modern factory town: they exist alongside of other influences, but they do not create the spirit of Western civilization, nor mould it into a definite philosophy of life. A Bible and shoe can be in the same box, but there is no casual connection between the two.

In like manner, modern Western civilization acknowledges that some respectability attaches itself to these devout souls, but it assumes and more often insists, that religion is for personal use, not social expression. Religion is regarded only as a pious appendage to life, not its soul; it sugar-coats political and economic activity, but does not infuse it. As Peguy has said: "Never has the temporal been so protected against the spiritual; and never has the spiritual been so unprotected against the temporal."

If anyone doubts the validity of this distinction between the individual Christians living in the Western world and the spirit of the Western world, let him suggest, for example, that the modern youth be given a religious and moral training in our schools. Immediately, the prophets of doom would arise in loud protest, cloaking hatred of religion under the pretext that there is "not sufficient time for religion," or that "we want no union of Church and State," or "religion is all right for the individual if he needs it, but it has no relation to politics or economics."

We must add to the distinction already made between the individual and society, the more important one between what is the good and the bad in any civilization, just as we distinguish between man and his disease. We regard the disease as evil, but the man as good. In an impersonal order, we make a distinction between the ship and its barnacles. The ship in its passage through the seas, develops barnacles which impede the free passage of the ship through the waters; it must occasionally be taken to dry dock to have the barnacles knocked away.

The ship is good; the barnacles are bad. Now the Western civilization, or what some call democracy, may be likened to a ship. America, in particular, is a good ship. It carries the precious cargo of the belief in inalienable rights and liberties, the value of the human person, representative government, and equal opportunities. It is freighted down also with the precious cargo of the Four Freedoms about which our President spoke: freedom of religion, freedom of speech, freedom from want and freedom from fear. It is freighted down also with the cargo of the right of sanctuary, for America has been in the past and is now a sanctuary for the persecuted as no other land on the face of God's earth has been a sanctuary. Finally, this ship is good for it is freighted down with the precious cargo of all those values which make us proud to call ourselves "Americans."

But it happens that this admirable ship of democracy has, in the course of the last century or more, accumulated certain barnacles. These barnacles are to be understood in terms of certain false assumptions which have too generally influenced much of our Western world. They have produced what Sorokin calls a Sensate Culture,[1] or what we will call a Secularist Culture, that is a culture in which the material and sensible values of life are divorced from their spiritual foundations. There is a grave danger that unless these barnacles are removed, the ship may sink.

These barnacles constitute what we have already called the passive or the soft barbarisms from within, and they are a danger to Western civilization—not quite as open as Totalitarianism, but just as insidious. All religious groups have warned us of the possibility of defeat from within through this materialism which, though it does not persecute religion, nevertheless abandons it.

The American Institute of Judaism, for example, on December 25, 1942, made this significant statement: "The failure of men to recognize the implications of the sovereignty of God and the sanctity of human life has resulted in moral disruption and worldwide devastation. Misreading the findings of the sciences, both physical and social, men have given their allegiance to false philosophies, spiritual and moral values have been divorced from human life and materialism has been made supreme in the affairs of men. In order to rebuild our broken civilization the spiritual

---

[1] P. A. Sorokin, "The Crisis of Our Age."

teachings of religion must become the foundations of the new world order and the dynamic force in a just and enduring peace."[2]

The Malvern Conference of the Church of England, on January 10, 1941, issued the same warning: "The war is not to be regarded as an isolated evil detached from the general condition of Western civilization during the last period. Rather it is to be seen as one symptom of a widespread disease and maladjustment resulting from the loss of conviction concerning the reality and character of God, and the true nature and destiny of Man."

The Federal Council of Churches of Christ of America, in the same spirit on April 15, 1941, stated: "We are well aware of the fact that in times like these Christians desire to be practical. . . . The Commission shares the desire, and has the intention to be practical, but we strongly disagree with the view that Christian principles have no practical relation to present-day problems. On the contrary, we trace many of our present troubles to political planning which was fatally defective precisely because it ignored Christian principles. We are confident that for the future only frustration can result if such precepts continue to be ignored."

Pius XII addressing himself to the world in his First Encyclical said that a loss of God had created a vacuum which no national or international myth could fill.

> In this atmosphere of alienation from God and
> de-Christianization, the thinking and planning,
> judgment and actions of men were bound to be-
> come materialistic and one-sided, to strive for mere

greatness and expansion of space, a boundless demand for increased possession of goods or power, a race for a quicker, richer and better production of all things which appeared to be conducive to material evolution and progress. These very symptoms appear in politics as an unlimited demand for expansion and political influence without regard to moral standards: in economic life they are represented by the predominance of mammoth concerns and trusts, in the social sphere it is the agglomeration of huge populations in cities and in the districts dominated by industry and trade, an agglomeration that is accompanied by the complete uprooting of the masses who have lost their standards of life, home, work, love, and hatred. By this new conception of thought and life, all ideas of social life have been impregnated with a purely mechanistic character.

Returning now to our theme: the ship is good, and the barnacles are bad; let us discuss the barnacles. These barnacles might be called superstitions or dogmas; in any case they are assumptions of sensate culture which the press, education, and public opinion accept as unchallenged truths.

The Superstition of Progress

The superstition of Progress asserts itself in some such fashion as this in our class rooms, best-sellers and high-class journals: Man is naturally good and indefinitely perfectible, and thanks to great cosmic floods of evolution will be swept forward and forward until he becomes a kind of god. Goodness increases with time, while evil and error decline. History represents the gradual but steady advance of man up the hill of the more abundant and happy life. No special institutions, no moral discipline, no Divine grace are necessary for the progress of man; for progress is automatic, due to the free play of natural forces and the operation of freedom in a world released from the superstition of religion. Because evil and sin are only vestigial remnants from the bestial past, evolution and science and education will finally eradicate them.

This superstition of Progress is false because it completely ignores the goal and purpose of progress. The modern world confuses motion with progress: instead of working toward an ideal, it changes the ideal and calls it progress. If every time an artist looked up he saw a different person sitting for the portrait, how would he ever know he was making any progress in painting? As Chesterton said: "There is one thing that never makes any progress and that is the idea of progress."

Progress in an indefinite future, but not beyond history, makes present moral lives meaningless and endows them with no other value than that of so many sticks to keep the cosmic bonfire blazing for the next generation. When the only kind of happiness men can enjoy is one which they celebrate in the distant future on the graves of their ancestors, then indeed their happiness is the happiness of grave diggers in the midst of a pestilence.

As Berdyaev so well expressed it: "Both from the religious and ethical points of view this positivist conception of progress is inadmissible, because by its very nature it excludes a solution to the tragic torments, conflicts and contradictions of life valid for all mankind, for all those generations who have lived and suffered. For it deliberately asserts that nothing but death and the grave awaits the vast majority of mankind and the endless succession of human generations throughout the ages, because they have lived in a tortured and imperfect state torn asunder

by contradictions. But somewhere on the peaks of historical destiny, on the ruins of preceding generations, there
shall appear the fortunate race of men reserved for the
bliss and perfection of integral life. All the generations that
have gone before are but the means to this blessed life, to
this blissful generation of the elect as yet unborn. . . . Thus
the religion of progress regards all the generations and epochs that have been as devoid of intrinsic value, purpose or
insignificance, as the mere means and instruments to the
ultimate goal.

"It is this fundamental moral contradiction that inval-
idates the doctrine of progress, turning it into a religion
of death instead of resurrection and eternal life. There is
no valid ground for degrading those generations whose lot
has been cast among pain and imperfection beneath that
whose pre-eminence has been ordained in blessedness and
joy. No future perfection can expiate the sufferings of past
generations. Such a sacrifice of all human destinies to the
messianic consummation of the favoured race can only revolt man's moral and religious conscience. A religion of
progress based on this apotheosis of a future fortunate generation is without compassion for either present or past; it
addresses itself with infinite optimism to the future, with
infinite pessimism to the past. It is profoundly hostile to the
Christian expectation of resurrection for all mankind, for
all the dead, fathers and forefathers.

"This Christian idea rests on the hope of an end to
historical tragedy and contradiction valid for all human
generations, and of resurrection in eternal life for all who
have ever lived. But the nineteenth-century conception of
progress admits to the messianic consummation only that
unborn generation of the elect to which all preceding generations have made their sacrifice. Such a consummation,

celebrated by the future elect among the graves of their ancestors, can hardly rally our enthusiasm for the religion of progress. Any such enthusiasm would be base and inappropriate."[3]

The doctrine of Progress confuses mechanical advancement with moral betterment. There is no denying the fact that there has been great progress in the material order, but mechanical development does not necessarily imply moral development. Progress in "things" is not necessarily progress in "persons." Planes may go faster, but man does not become happier. Progress in medicine is not necessarily progress in ethics, and mastery over disease is not necessarily mastery over sin. Conquest of nature does not mean conquest of selfishness. Scientific advancement is no guarantee of moral betterment. Greater power over nature can increase our potentiality for evil. Put the forces of evil in charge of radio, the press and the new inventions and you corrupt or destroy a nation. Mechanics is one thing, freedom is quite another. Moral optimism, based on mechanical progress and the assumption of the natural goodness of man, understands neither the heights to which man can climb through the grace of God, nor the depths to which he can fall through the abandonment of a Divine life purchased through a cross. The conquest of nature does not parallel our conquest of evil. We are equipped like giants to subdue the environment of the air and the sea and the bowels of the earth, but we are as weak as pigmies for the conquest of ourselves. The greater power which science has put into man's hands can, unless his will is right, increase his potentiality for evil, as the present chaos so well bears witness. Time does not always operate in favor

---

[3] Nicholas Berdyaev, *The Meaning of History*, pp. 188–90 (1936).

of human betterment; because a man is sick, time does not necessarily make him better. Unless evil is corrected, time operates in favor of disease, decay and death.

The superstition of Progress denies human responsibility. When human goodness is attributed to automatic laws of nature, but never to good will; when evil is explained in terms of environment, heredity, bad milk, insufficient playgrounds and those naughty ductless glands, but never to a perverse order, then the world is most in danger of losing freedom when it talks about it.

Someone was recently horrified at the immorality of young girls between the ages of fifteen and seventeen and suggested that the solution to this problem was to "build more dance halls where they sold soft drinks."

If we attribute evil to external circumstances, and believe that we can cultivate virtue by a swing band and soda pop, we will have become a nation where there is no freedom because there is no responsibility. Evil is not in the absence of opportunities for amusement. Evil is in the will, and in the heart and in the decisions of each and every one of us. Youth can be vicious with dance halls; it can be virtuous without them, but youth will never be good unless its will is ordered to the moral law of the holy God. The confusion of the idea of progress with the idea of evolution, kills the value of intention and the fruits of high resolves. True progress is ethically and not cosmically conditioned; it depends not on the refinement of luxuries, but in their deliberate control through human intention. There is really therefore only one true progress in the world and that consists in the diminution of the traces of original sin.

Historical facts do not support the Utopian illusion that goodness increases with time. What happens in reality is something quite different. Evil grows along with the

good. The history of the world is rather like a tension between good and evil than an escalator which keeps going
upwards. "The kingdom of heaven is likened to a man that
sowed good seed in his field. But while men were asleep,
his enemy came and oversowed cockle among the wheat
and went his way. And when the blade sprang up and had
brought forth fruit, then appeared also the cockle. And the
servants of the goodman of the house coming said to him,
'Sir, didst thou not sow good seed in thy field? Whence
then hath it cockle?' And he said to them, 'An enemy hath
done this.' And the servants said to him, 'Wilt thou that we
go and gather it up?' And he said, 'No, lest perhaps gathering up the cockle, you root up the wheat also together
with it. Suffer both to grow until the harvest, and in the
time of the harvest I will say to the reapers: gather up first
the cockle and bind it into bundles to burn, but the wheat
gather ye into my barn'" (Matthew 13: 24–30).

Nothing better proves the fallacy of progress than to
recall the interval between modern wars. It has been a
common fashion for the Utopians to explain wars away
as "falls in the evolutionary process," or as "necessary in-
cidents in the evolution from savagery to civilization," or
as "survivals of the animal in civilized man." But history
does not prove we are making progress; instead of evolv-
ing from savagery to civilization, we seem to be devolving
from civilization to savagery. The interval between the Na-
poleonic war and the Franco-Prussian war was fifty-five
years; the interval between the Franco-Prussian war and
the first World War was forty-three years; and the interval
between the first World War and this one was twenty-one
years. Fifty-five, forty-three, twenty-one years—and each
war more destructive than the former, and at a time when
man materially had more to make for happiness than any

other period of history. Is that progress? Shall we not learn from our modern history its record that man, once he forgets his God, has also an increasing capacity for evil.

The sad and tragic fact is that modern man under sufficient stress, and even amidst comforts spiced with lust, will do deeds of evil as terrible as anyone recorded in history. Barbarism is not behind us; it is beneath us. And it can emerge at any moment unless our wills, aided by the grace of God, repress it. The modern superstition of man's indefinite perfectibility, without God's sustaining graces, forgets the historical data before our eyes, that history is creating ever-increasing possibilities for chaos and wars. Our mechanical progress in moving quickly can go hand in hand with power to do more evil. Let no one deny it: our scientific progress has outstripped our moral progress. We are a more comfortable people than our ancestors, but are we necessarily a happier people? The myth of necessary progress is exploded. But that is no reason why the Liberals who were so optimistic about Progress, like Bertrand Russell, should now fall into a hellish despair. Because the evil in the world does not evolve right does not mean there is no right. It only means that we have to put the evil right, and in order to do this we may have to learn the lesson of a cross and the toil of Gethsemane. Neither is the solution to be found among those Fascist intelligentsia who appeal to the authority of H. G. Wells and requote in the darkness of their souls: "Men are borne along through space and time regardless of themselves, as if to the awakening greatness of Men."[4]

The answer is somewhere else. Maybe we had better get back again to God.

---

[4] H. G. Wells, *The Work, Wealth and Happiness of Mankind* (1931).

The Superstition of Scientism

By the superstition of Scientism we do not mean science, but rather that particular abuse of it which affirms that the scientific method is, as John Dewey put it, "The sole authentic mode of revelation." For the modern sensate mind, to understand is to measure; to know is to count. The senses are the only sources of knowledge. Hence any knowledge derived from any source other than courting and experimentation is illusory. Sensible knowledge is the final arbiter of experience. Science says "this," or science says "that," is the last word to be said on any subject. Hence there is no place for values, tradition, metaphysics, revelation, faith, authority, or theology. God has no purposes in the universe; first of all because there is no God, and secondly, because there are no purposes. Scientism does not say we ignore purposes in our laboratory, but rather we eliminate purposes from the universe. The greatest obstacle to progress, according to Dewey, is the survival of old institutions such as the Church, and the best guarantee of freedom in the world is the spread of the scientific method. Wherever there is science there is freedom, he declares. Or, as Russell puts it, wherever there is science there is culture. Such is the superstition of Scientism.

Science is a very valid and necessary way of knowing, but only of knowing those things which are subject to experimentation and to the methods of a laboratory. The great values of life such as justice, truth, and charity are beyond such an experimentation. No one yet has ever been able to put a mother's love into a test tube, and yet who will deny its reality. Nor can we throw a man into a caldron to boil to see if he gives forth the unmistakable green fumes of envy and jealousy.

Once the modern mind denied that man was a creature made in the image and likeness of God, it naturally fell into the error of saying that man was made in the image and likeness of the beast. Man then ceased to be studied theologically or philosophically and began to be studied with the other sciences of nature, biology, physiology and physics. But this identification of man with nature deprived man of all value. Once you make man a cog in a vast astronomical machine, or a molecule in a spatio-temporal continuum, or an enlarged cell of some original protoplasmic stuff, you deny that man has a right to be treated differently than anything in nature. But, if man is not different from nature, then what value has man? If there is no specific difference between a man and a horse, then why not yoke man to the plow of Nazism or the tractor of Marxian Socialism, or make him an instrument of the State as the Fascist intelligentsia teach today.

The answer to this superstition of Scientism, which makes man meaningless by making him one with nature, is not in the repudiation of science but in the recognition that there are higher values beyond the ken of science. Professor Hocking, of Harvard University, speaking of Scientism says, "This desiccated picture of the world is a damnable lie—for values are there; values are among the inescapable facts of the world—and whoever disseminates this death's-head world-view in the schools and colleges of this or any other land is disseminating falsehood with the browbeaten connivance of a whole herd of intellectual sheep, and of culpable guardians of the young. . . . This is one of the insights with which the new era of History begins."[5]

Scientism has ruined higher education in the United States by prostrating itself before the god of counting, and by assuming that anyone who has counted something that

[5] W. E. Hocking, *What Man can Make of Man*, p. 33 (Harpers, 1942).

has never been counted before is a learned man. It makes no difference what you count, but in the name of heaven, count! A certain western university has awarded a Doctor of Philosophy degree for a thesis on the "Microbic Content of Cotton Undershirts." A mid-western university has counted the ways of washing dishes; and some eastern universities have counted the infinitives in Augustine, the datives in Ovid, and the four ways of cooking ham; while another counted the "psychological reactions of the post-rotational eye-movement of squabs."

These subjects seem amusing when extracted from the context of universities, but the universities unfortunately take them seriously. The result is we are giving our students theories, opinions and facts which will be out of date before the ink on the diploma fades; but we are not equipping them for life by proposing its high purposes. In the madness of specialization we have come to know more and more about less and less, but in the meantime we have lost ourselves in the maze of numbers. Fed with huge quantities of undigested facts, our judgment has become hampered and we have only unrelated bits of information instead of wisdom which alone is true knowledge. Go into any parochial school in the United States, take out a child in the first or second grade and ask him: "Who made you?" "What is the purpose of life?" "Are you different from an animal?" Any such child aged seven or eight could answer the question of the purpose of life. But ask a Ph.D. graduate, who has counted the microbes on cotton undershirts, why he is here or where he is going; he could not tell you. He would not have a five-cent-gadget in his house five minutes without knowing its purpose, but he would live ten, twenty or sixty years without knowing why he is here, or where he is going. What is the use of living unless we know the purpose of being a man? It is not true, as is so often asserted, that modern youth is revolutionary because he has lacked sufficient economic advantages. Never in the history of the world did youth have so many advantages. The modern youth is revolutionary because hc has no purpose in life and hence doubts the worthwhileness of living amidst plenty. Anything that loses its purpose becomes revolutionary. When a boiler loses its purpose it explodes; when a man loses his purpose he revolts.

Is it true, as Dr. Dewey has said, that the use of the scientific method is the guarantee of freedom? What country, before this world war began, was generally recognized as the most advanced in the scientific method? To what nation of the world did our American universities look as the paragon of scientific perfection, and from which did they draw their greatest scientific inspiration? It was from Germany. And yet there is no country in the world where freedom is more universally suppressed.

Is it true, as a Mr. Russell affirms, that if you spread science you spread culture? We gave Japan science. But will these philosophers of the superstition of Scientism dare assert that culture went with it? The scientific method did not bring to a benighted people an increase of tolerance and kindness and brotherhood. They have proven what we ought to recognize; namely, that a high degree of scientific advancement can exist with utter and absolute moral depravity.

We are paying the penalty for divorcing our science from God. Nature, which science studies, belongs to God, and when man turns against God nature or science turns against man. Francis Thompson beautifully spoke of this when he found that the whole world turned against him because he would not answer the call of God:

I tempted all His servitors, but to find
My own betrayal in their constancy,
In faith to Him their fickleness to me,
Their traitorous trueness, and their loyal deceit.[6]

That is the true story: Nature will be false to anyone
who is untrue to its Maker. I am free to break the law of
gravitation but if I do, the law breaks me. The law still
stands. I am free to ignore God the Creator of nature,
but if I do, nature will wreck me. For years science has
been discovering the wonders of nature, finding in the
tiny atom a miniature of the great solar system. But, instead of glorifying God for the order, law, and harmony
they found in His universe, scientists vainly assumed that
because they discovered the laws they were the authors
of the Book of Nature, instead of only its proof-readers.
Tearing nature away from God, nature now turned
against man; refusing to serve God, nature refused to
serve man. The result is that science which was supposed
to be our servant is now our master. Why do millions in
the world shrink in terror from a machine in the air? Why
does man use his technique to destroy man? Why do children crouch in dread and mothers dig like moles into the
bowels of the earth as bombs fall from the skies, as all hell
is let loose, if it is not because something has got out of
our control?

Science has become a source of destruction, because
we refused to use it as a means for lifting us to God. It is not
that God has punished man for his ingratitude to nature;
it is rather that nature, in unconscious loyalty, has punished man for his disloyalty. No creature can be used for

---

[6] *Hound of Heaven.*

the happiness of man, which has alienated itself from the service to its Creator.

Something else that we have forgotten in our glorification of science as the only true knowledge, is that science itself has no morality. An isosceles triangle for example is no more moral than a square; vitamins may be more hygienic than the pointer-readings, but they are not more ethical. The morality of science is derived from the purpose for which it is used. But in denying all purposes in life, we have made science its own justification. If there is no higher knowledge than science, how will we know what is good or bad? Hitler, using science, spreads tyranny on a vast scale and suppresses human rights and liberties through new weapons which science puts into his hands. How shall we say he is unmoral and we, who use science to defend liberties, are moral, unless there be a standard outside of both? Cannot we see that by making science an ultimate, we have deprived ourselves of a criterion by which to judge our cause from theirs? Divorce the products of science from the higher objectives of human life which reason and faith reveal to us, and you have a mad world wherein "humanity preys upon itself like monsters of the deep."

The Superstition of Relativism

The superstition of Relativism tells us there is no distinction between truth and error, right and wrong; everything depends upon one's point of view. All values are relative and depend entirely upon the way people live in any generation. If in the twentieth century they live monogamously, then monogamy is right; if in the future, they live polygamously, then polygamy is right. Whatever the majority decides is right, and a Gallup Poll is the best way to find it out. When expedient, moral conventions can be accepted;

when a hindrance, they can be rejected. There are no objective moral standards; no absolute distinction between good and evil. Everyone is his own law-giver; everyone is his own judge. Tolerance is the greatest virtue and tolerance means indifference to truth and error, right and wrong. Such is Relativism.

The superstition of Relativism, or the notion that there is no absolute distinction between right and wrong, springs in this country from the philosophy of Pragmatism. This philosophy denied that God was an Absolute; it judged truth not by its consistency, nor its correspondence with reality, but by its utility. In the words of one of its best known exponents: Truth is to be judged by its "cash value in terms of a particular experience." "The gods we stand by are the gods we need and can use." "The 'true' to put it very briefly, is only the expedient in the way of thinking, just as the 'right' is only the expedient in the way of our behaving, expedient in almost any fashion. In other words, whatever succeeds is right."

This particular philosophy was born of an excessive adoration of the scientific method. Science evolved practical prescriptions for dealing with particular problems; when the practical problems changed, the prescription changed. This method was practical in dealing with phenomena, but the philosopher enlarged it to apply to all truth. Nothing was considered immutable or changeable. Everything was relative to a point of view. Not being able to apply his method to religion and morals, instead of acknowledging the insufficiency of his method, the pragmatist denied the value of religion and morals.

The pragmatists thus assume that the spiritual and moral needs of man and a nation needed no other foundation than that of the utilitarian activities associated with earning a living. Ideas thus were regarded as instruments of power. These ideas—that there is no absolute distinction between truth and error, right and wrong, that morality is determined by the subjective outlook of every individual and is devoid of all objective standards,—are taught in many secular colleges and universities in the United States. A distinguished professor in a mid-western university revealed that there was not a single student in his class who could give a rational justification for democracy. The students justified democracy solely on the grounds of expediency and the fact that it had the greatest power; none saw any intrinsic value in democracy. Very few saw the evil implications in a morality of self-advantage, and some who did were reluctant to abandon it in a world where success was the measure of greatness. It took a great catastrophe to bring home its falsity. And this is how it happened.

What moral standards are the Japanese violating, if the criterion of truth and righteousness is expediency? Why do we say that Japan has violated the conscience of the world, if the conscience of the world has no other measure than the useful? Incidentally, where was this moral conscience of the world before the war began? How shall the rightness of our cause be distinguished from the rightness of our enemies, if there is no objective standard outside of both? If there is no right and wrong, independent of the whims of individuals, how shall we defend ourselves against despotism? The ultimate bulwark of democracy is in the recognition of moral standards, so absolute that citizens are willing in the end, if need be, to give everything—even life—to maintain them. If there is no objective distinction between right and wrong, how can Hitler be wrong? How can he be right?

Our journalists, our educators, our movies, our best sellers, our forums, and even some of the Churches have been sniping away for years at the moral law, knocking off first its application to politics and economics, and then to the family, then the individual. They have sneered at and ridiculed those who still held on to the moral law, calling them "reactionary," "behind the times," and labelling purity and truthfulness as "bourgeois virtues" in the language of Marx. They now say that all we need do about evil is to forget it, and that faith and morality can be brought back into civilization as one might buy a commodity at a drugstore.

We have an active barbarism to defeat on the outside, and we have a passive barbarism from within; the first is openly violent, the second is sinister and secretive. The first endangers our shores, the second pollutes our souls; the first would take away external liberties such as freedom of speech and press, and the second would take away internal liberty, or the right to call our soul our own. The first makes us stronger, by the mere fact that we resist; the second makes us weaker by the mere fact that like a cancer we are blind to its dangers. We could defeat the enemy on the outside, and still completely collapse from the inside. We could win the war and lose peace. "Fear ye not them that kill the body and are not able to kill the soul: but rather fear him that can destroy both soul and body in hell" (Mt. 10:28).

When Colin Kelly as a selfless pilot sank the first Japanese ship of this war and in doing so lost his life; when Edward O'Hara shot down the first Japanese plane; when Dick Fleming made himself the first human torpedo; when Daniel O'Callaghan became the first admiral to go down fighting on the bridge of the *San Francisco*: when Mike Moran became the first naval officer to sink six Japanese ships in single combat; when Commander Shea became the first fighting man whose last letter to his son became a famous testament on patriotism; when the five Sullivans became the first American family of boys to be snuffed out in this war; these men had no "opinion" about America's cause; they did not believe that the righteousness of the stars and stripes depended upon this subjective outlook. They believed in an absolute distinction between right and wrong, our cause and our enemy; in fact, so much did they believe in it that life was secondary to that cause. And while these and millions of men in our armed forces believe in such an absolute distinction between right and wrong, our Fascist intelligentsia are telling us: "right and wrong are relative to expediency; it all depends upon your point of view." Nonsense! It does not! Our cause is right! It is right before God! It is right under God! And in God's name we will defend it!

The Superstition of Materialism

The superstition of Materialism affirms that man has no soul, that there is no future life, and that man has no other destiny than that of the animals. Being devoid of spirit man may best be described not as a creature made to the image and likeness of God but as a "psychoanalytical bag with physiological libido," or a "stimulus response mechanism."

Since there is no future life, it follows that the good life consists in material improvement; that civilization and culture vary in direct ratio with wealth and the two chickens in every pot; that want is the greatest cause of misery and unhappiness, and that abundance is the surest guarantee of peace and happiness. Goodness, truth, honor, and beauty are natural by-products of the increase of national dividends. The end of life is the acquisition of money, the

ceaseless enjoyment of pleasure, and the avoidance of sacrifice. Such is the superstition of Materialism.

It simply is not true that peace follows material prosperity, and unhappiness follows the want of it; rather
unhappiness flows from loss of a goal and purpose of life
through the denial of the human soul. It is not economic
hardship nor political injustice which has driven modern
man to revolutionary action: it is the horror of an empty
sterile world. Men lived with only the necessities of life
before, but they were never as revolutionary as they are
today. Religious communities throughout the Church survive on the minimum of existence, with vows of poverty,
chastity and obedience, and where shall you find greater
happiness? The major frustrations of life are not economic.
Glance around at those who possess abundance of material goods. Does happiness increase with wealth? There is
more frustration among the rich than the poor. It is the
former who are most addicted to selfishness, who are sati-
ated and unhappy. Sin and evil do not disappear with the
advent of gold. Society can become inhuman while preserving all the advantages of great material prosperity.

The materialist superstition that man has no other
end than this life, and no other task than economic betterment, and that education must produce a race of doers
rather than an "impractical" race of knowers, will eventu-
ally build a civilization in which we will have no standards
to judge what is economically good or socially bad. The
philosopher could make a good world without an economist, but the economist could not make one without the
philosopher. By making acquisitiveness supreme, we lose
all standards of knowing what is right or wrong. Social reform then has no other inspiration than envy. As Tawney
says of them: "They denounce, and rightly, the injustices

of capitalism; but they do not always realize that capitalism is maintained not only by capitalists but by those who, like some of themselves, would be capitalists if they could, and that these injustices survive, not merely because the rich exploit the poor, but because in their hearts too many of the poor admire the rich. They know and complain that they are tyrannized over by the power of money. But they do not yet see that what makes money the tyrant of society is largely their own reverence of it." And to complete Tawney's picture, if we make material standards the only standards, then we become incapable of judging the new acquisitive society which is arising—the acquisitiveness of power. As fortunes dwindle, as taxes eat up inheritances, and as bureaucracies begin to administer vast sums of money formerly administered by capitalists and bankers, envious, greedy and lustful men will seek to become dispensers of that social booty, and who shall say that these new financiers of power are wrong? Given no standards other than materialism, wherein remorse is disjoined from power, we will have a new capitalism—the capitalism of power, wherein the bureaucrats become the bankers.

> Bidding the law make court'sy to their will;
> Hooking both right and wrong to the appetite,
> To follow as it draws![7]

The modern man wants back his soul! He wants the intelligentsia to stop the nonsense of regarding him as an animal, a libido, a tool-maker, or a voter and to begin to look at him as a creature made in the image and likeness of God.

---

[7] Shakespeare, *Measure for Measure*.

It is pathetic to hear people asking: "What can I as an individual do in this crisis?" So many feel that they are like robots in a great machine, that they would like to get away from it all, even if it meant climbing back into the Catacombs. Like the Jews in exile they hang their harps on the trees, and ask how can they sing a song without a soul.

In plain, simple language, all these individuals want their souls back! They want to be whole again. They are sick of being thrown into a Darwinian pot to boil as a beast, or into a Freudian stew to squirm as a libido, or thrust into the Marxian sandwich to be squeezed between two conflicting slices of capital and labor. They want to possess that which makes them human, gives meaning to politics, economics, psychology, sociology; namely, the soul.

Listen to them: "I want my soul back; that I may be free from earth; that I may surrender it to Him. I want to hold my own life, as a responsible creature, in my own hands, that I may emancipate it not only from Nature, but even from the man-made environment. Somewhere I am lost amid organized chaos. Everywhere I hear talk about freedom, but how can I be free unless I have a soul? Stones are not free; neither are cows or cabbages. From every side I am told I have no soul. If I have no soul, then I have nothing to lose, and if I have nothing to lose why should I feel unhappy when I sin?

"In my misery I go to the modern world and it tells me that I need to be integrated with society, and hence I must throw myself into the vast social experiences and sociological adventurings. But society cannot help me, for it is in the same mess as I. Society is made up of millions of frustrated souls exactly like myself. How can it cure me, when it has the same disease? Then the world tells me I should have ideals, for no one can live without faith; give yourself over to aims, and you will find your soul. But when I ask whether these ideals are real, such as God and the moral law, I am told that they are myths; that it makes no difference whether there is a God, or whether Christ ever lived, or that there is any reason behind these ideals; but that they are just helpful fictions.

"I am thus back to where I was at the beginning. I am told I should have faith, but the world can give me none; I am told to have ideals and at the same time told that they are only fictions. I am not an animal, not a libido, not a proletarian, not an atom; I am something else, more and greater than these things. And I want to be more! I want back my soul!"[8]

To get back our souls we have to turn our backs on all the twaddle we have been fed for the last century about the nature of man. We might just as well put it bluntly, and say that what we call modern is only an old error with a new label. The modern view of man is wrong—completely and absolutely wrong, and if we go on following it we will end in blind alleys, frustrated hopes and unhappy existences. It is not nearly as funny as we thought to make a monkey out of a man.

The millions of our boys on the battlefronts of the world, fighting for their lives and for great moral issues, will recover their souls. Amidst wounds of death, fire and shell, they will get close to the meaning of life and to that something within them that makes them human. They will be angry when they look back on the way some of them were educated. They will come to hate not only the enemy they meet in battle, but the intelligentsia who told them they were only animals. They will begin to realize that these

---

[8] W. E. Hocking, *op. cit.*, pp. 52 ff.

intelligentsia robbed them of their greatest possession—faith. For a while they will wander around the battlefields like Magdalene in the Garden saying: "They have taken away my Lord, and I know not where they laid Him." But when they do stumble on Him as Magdalene did when she saw the livid marks of the nails, they will enter once again into the possession of the soul. And when they come marching home there will be a judgment on those who told them they had no soul; they will live like new men and they will give a rebirth to America under God.

Recovering our souls demands doing two things: turning our backs completely on the way the modern world thinks, and facing our Divine Original, Who made us and Who alone can tell us what we are. Instead of drifting with the current into the abyss of hopeless paganism, we must learn to swim against it like the salmon back to the spawning ground where man is born again.

> It is the Soul's prerogative, its fate,
> To shape the outward to its own estate.
> If right itself, then all around is well;
> If wrong, it makes of all without a hell,
> So multiplies the Soul its joys and pain,
> Gives out itself, itself takes back again.
> Transformed by Thee, the world hath but one face.[9]

The Superstition of License

The superstition of License here means perverted freedom. It defines freedom as the right to do whatever you please or the absence of law, restraint, and discipline. A man is considered free when his desires are satisfied; he is

---

[9] R. H. Dana, "Thoughts on The Soul."

not free when they are unsatisfied. The goal of freedom is
self-expression. Such is the superstition of License.

This superstition is grounded on a false definition of
freedom. Freedom does not mean the right to do whatever we please. If it did, it would be a physical power, not
a moral power. Certainly, we can do whatever we please,
but ought we? Freedom means the right to do whatever
we ought, and therefore is inseparable from law. It was
precisely because we made freedom consist in the right to
do whatever we pleased, that we produced a civilization
which was nothing but a criss-cross of individual egotisms in the economic, political and international order.
Communism, Nazism and Fascism arose to organise that
chaos and became as so many convulsive attempts to arrest a disintegration by the false method of going to the
other extreme, by extinguishing all freedom in order to
preserve law.

The solution lies along other lines, namely that we are
most free when we act within the law and not outside it. An
aviator is most free to fly when he obeys the law of gravitation. As Our Lord said: "The truth will make you free."

Nor is it true that freedom consists in the shaking-off
of convention and tradition and authority. What is called
self-expression is in reality often nothing else than self-
destruction. The railroad engine that suddenly becomes so
"progressive" that it will not follow the tracks laid out by
an engineer of a previous generation soon discovers that it
is not "free" to be an engine at all. If freedom means only
the lessening of authority, then we shall have indeed the
thrill of risk, but in the end we shall have no freedom. As
Leo XIII expressed it, "liberty will ever be more free and
secure, in proportion as license is kept in restraint."

About the only curbs which the sensate man allows himself are those which contribute to his own physical well-being. Dieting is about the only discipline left, and dieting is not fasting. Dieting is for the body; fasting is for the soul. Moral restraints, spiritual discipline, ascetic life, denial of evil thoughts and temptations, restraint in the use of the legitimate pleasures of life—these things are meaningless to the modern man who feels he has sufficient warrant in throwing off moral standards for no other reason than because they are old. When we reach a point where we measure our self-expression by the height of the pile of our discarded disciplines, inhibitions, and moral standards, then anyone who would die to preserve that disemboweled ghost of liberty is a fool.

Salvation lies in the fact that freedom exists for a purpose; that is, we have freedom to give it away. No one keeps his freedom. A man in love surrenders it to the woman he loves and calls it a "sweet slavery"; the modern man who has thrown off morality surrenders it to public opinion, becomes the slave of fashion and passing moods; the Christian who uses his freedom gives it to God, "to serve Whom is to reign" and then purchases the slavery of the Infinite in Whom is Love and Life and Truth. Every freedom is for the sake of bondage, and we are all in bondage—to a fellow creature, to the mob, to Hitler, or to God Who alone can make us truly free.

That is why freedom for freedom's sake is meaningless. I want to be free from something, only because I want to be free for something. That is why freedom is inseparable from purpose. Freedom from restraint is justified only when it depends on freedom for something else. The fallacy of the superstition of License is that it makes us free just to be free, which is as meaningless and as unsatisfying as a cold in the head.

The superstition of License assumes that men will always do the right thing if they are educated; hence they need no restraint and no discipline. And here we touch on the basic weakness of Sensate education; namely, it assumes that sin is due to ignorance and not to the abuse of freedom. When evil was attributed to the will, the school belonged to the Church. Now that we believe there is no sin, and that what we call evil is only want of enlightenment, the school stands in isolation from religion and morality. Schools once belonged to religious groups in order that moral training of the will might keep pace with enlightenment of the intellect. Now the universities have for the most part lost all concern for the will. When confronted with the problem of evil, they immediately rush to a conference to discuss greater knowledge, when what is really needed is more discipline.

The Sensate culture is right in saying that sin is irrational because every sin is a violation of a law of Eternal Reason, but the unreason or ignorance is not the citadel of sin. A man sins, not because he is ignorant, but because he is perverse. The intellect makes mistakes, but the will sins. A man may know all we teach him and still be a bad man; the intelligentsia are not necessarily the saints. The ignorant are not necessarily devils. Enlightenment and education can become the servants of a perverse will, and when they do it is like hell being let loose. Unless a man's will has a purpose and it is a good one, education will do nothing for him except to fortify his own egotism.

There is an almost unpardonable naivete about those who say that reason alone can conquer anarchic impulses. Rather, the reverse is true. Reason can be used just as easily to justify evil, to rationalize evil, to destroy supernatural truths and, in the form of science, to invent lethal instruments for the defence of those wicked tendencies in time of war.

Reason was made to lead us to faith as the senses were made to lead us to reason. Now when reason is torn up from its roots in God, how can we trust its conclusions? If chance, blind evolution, or chaos were its origin, then why should it now be expected to be anything less than chaotic, unstable and fluid? An age which has put all its trust in enlightenment as the cure of evil has found itself possessed of the greatest evil and war in the history of the world.

These superstitions constitute the cult of our contemporary Western Civilization. The chaos into which they have led us reveals their fallacies more effectively than any intellectual argument. The so-called progressive man, who today is bewildered, baffled and depressed at the disorder in the world need only go into his own godless disordered interior life to find its secret; the man without moral standards and therefore chaotic is the miniature of the world without a moral standard and therefore at war.

If these superstitions still exercise some influence, it is only because of artificial respiration given them by two classes of reactionaries—economic reactionaries and intellectual reactionaries.

The economic reactionaries are those who believe that any system which enables them to get rich must necessarily be a good system; hence any change in the existing order they regard as radicalism, revolutionism or Communism.

The intellectual reactionaries are the intelligentsia (we use that word to distinguish them from true intellectuals). By the intelligentsia we mean those who have been educated beyond their intelligence. Like the economic reactionaries they equate what they have with what is best, the difference being that their wealth is ideological, not

material. Their clichés, catch-words, and ideologies have
value only in a world of a chaos which produced two world
wars in twenty-one years; but they would be without validity any other time or in any other order based on justice
and charity. They would be just as out of place in such a
world as a teeter-totter in an old folks' home. A high-school
youngster who thinks the "Jersey Bounce" is the highest
expression of music would be lost at a concert of Toscanini.

Despite these two reactionary forces, it should now be
recognized that these superstitions have failed to provide
an adequate dynamic for either peace or war. The longer
we try to keep them alive, the ruder will be our awakening;
the more terrible will be our judgment.

It is no answer to retort with the old cliché that religion
has been the enemy of science, for he who has eyes can
see that science today is the enemy of man. It is not religion which has tyrannized man. Science has its place in the
world; this we not only admit—this we insist upon. But its
place is not at the peak of the pyramid of knowledge where
Descartes placed it when he enthroned mathematics, or
where Kant placed it when he enthroned physics, and
where Comte placed it when he enthroned sociology. That
place belongs to theology, the one science which makes a
university, for as the word "university" implies all knowledge and all sciences and all arts turn on one axis, which
is God. Cardinal Newman in his masterly treatise, "The
Idea of a University" allowed the imagination to run riot
by picturing a university of the future where there would
be no theology. To bring home the horror of such a condition, he described it as follows: "Henceforth, man is to
be as if he were not, in the general course of Education;
the moral and mental sciences are to have no professional
chairs, and the treatment of them is to be left as a matter

of private judgment, which each individual may carry out as he will. I can just fancy such a prohibition abstractly possible; but one thing I cannot fancy possible, *viz.:* that the parties in question, after this sweeping act of exclusion, should henceforth send out proposals on the basis of such exclusion for publishing an Encyclopedia, or erecting a National University."

But these conditions are upon us now, and so strongly entrenched is the opposition that to plead for a return of theology to university curricula would be to bring down upon one's head the wrath of those intelligentsia who still live in the Dark Ages and still feed on the superstition that the proper way to study man is to study nature. Some day under the pressure of catastrophe we will come to see that as science reveals nature, so theology reveals man. In that day, universities will be universities.

In this conflict we must not save everything just as it is nor seek to maintain the *status quo*, nor preserve an empire, nor get back the kind of a world that existed before this war began, for if we did we would be fighting to keep a world from whose womb came the satellites of anti-Christ: Hitler and Hirohito and others.

Some things are not worth fighting for. One of these things is an unredeemed, materialistic selfish order, organized on the basis of neglect of God and the abandonment of moral standards. The victors who won the war of 1918 lost the peace because they attempted to keep a world together on the basis of the outworn slogans and the really bad philosophy of the French Revolution. Our peacemakers, inspired more by the expiring convulsions of a liberal world born 150 years before, became blinded to the needs of a new world expressed in the protests of the revolutions of Germany, Italy and Russia. We won the war because we were stronger; we lost the peace because we tried to keep everything together on the basis of the liberalistic, capitalistic, individualistic, irreligious world of the outworn nineteenth century.

Napoleon carried the ideas of the French Revolution over Europe. Hitler carried the ideas of Marx over Europe. Both have done a service. Both swept away the litter of a bad world; one a monarchical world based on privilege of power, the other the capitalistic world based on the privilege of money. Both are wrong. He who would will to keep either privilege of power or money will keep only the dynamite for the next world war. We are not out to preserve either the Marxian or the French Revolution—we are at war this time to build an order not for the common man, spoon-fed by democracies, but for common service to a common good: a world of free men—free from economic want and therefore free to save their souls. This is worth fighting for!

When the ship is sinking, we must not think of the cargo. It is not the ship of democracy nor the ship of America, nor the ship of our Four Freedoms we must abandon. But the barnacles we must abandon. Our task is not the restoration of everything as it was; restoration could be our greatest obstacle to peace. It is regeneration we are seeking. No sane person would suggest that when this war is over London should rebuild its bombed buildings just exactly as they were, just as no sane person would suggest the restoration of a world which in fifteen years vomited three terrific revolutions: red, brown and black. Nor would he suggest that we re-establish the same old boundaries, the same sovereignties the same anemic League of Nations. Blind indeed would anyone be who suggests that we preserve the present order. There is one other order and that is our hope—the Christian order which starts with man.

CHAPTER FOUR

The Revolution of Man

For years Lenin, Mussolini and Hitler were saying that the old order was dead. We ridiculed them, insisting that the liberalistic, capitalistic, agnostic world of the nineteenth century with its business and education on the table, and its morals and religion on the sideboard to sugar-coat them when necessary, would never die. Lenin, Mussolini and Hitler were right in saying that the old order was dead. But they were wrong in saying that the new order or the future would be theirs, namely, socialism of class, nation and race. Our error has been to assume that the choice is between their new order based on socialism, and our old order based on individualism. It is not. There is still another order of which the modern mind never thinks, because it has had no contact with genuine Christianity in over two hundred years, and that is the Christian order.

These totalitarian heresies were protests against an old order, for example: Marxian Socialism reacted against defects in Capitalism; Fascism reacted against defects in

Parliamentarianism; Nazism reacted against defects in Nationalism, as in the League of Nations. Because they were protests against an old order, they practically never embodied a wholeness of view; their character was determined by the errors they combatted. For that reason, Marxian Socialism is nothing but rotted Capitalism on a State basis; Fascism is nothing but rotted Parliamentarianism on a one-party basis; Nazism is nothing but rotted Nationalism on a racial basis. In each case, they took their position from the enemy. They were inspired more by a hatred of something they wished to overthrow than by a love of the new ideals which they desired to establish.

Because political and economic revolutions were rebellions against the last revolution, they tended to bestow an absolutely sacred character on previously neglected elements of the régime they sought to overthrow. That is why we have capital in the saddle in one revolution, labor in the saddle in the next revolution, and poor John Q. Public hitch-hiking but never getting a ride. We need an entirely different kind of revolution, one that will not keep its eye on the last revolution nor take its character from it, but will concentrate on man in its highest reaches and noblest destiny. This is the Christian revolution.

The Christian world-view differs from the totalitarian and the old materialist culture of the Western World in one basic fact: it believes that it is man who makes society, and not society which makes man. That is why the first discussion of the Christian order must begin with man.

After all, what is the use of a revolution or a new system of economics or a new international society, unless we know the type of creature who will live in it?

For the last century the world has had a very distorted notion of man. In fact there were fashions in man as there were in clothes. Each fashion concentrated on one aspect of man to the neglect of all the others, like the five blind men who felt an elephant, each describing it differently accordingly as he touched its trunk, the tail, the ear and so forth.

In the Days of Darwin, blind thinkers went to man and since he felt like an animal they said he must be an animal. Thus we had jurists like Justice Holmes of the Supreme Court defining man as a "cosmic ganglion." If man is only a ganglion why should we go to war to prevent Hitler from making mincemeat of ganglia?

Then came the new fashion. Blind men felt man and found that he was made up of nerves, reflexes and responses, so they defined man as a "physiological bag filled with psychological libido," as they consulted dream books after each fitful sleep to learn what Freud had to say about their sex life.

Then came another blind philosopher, that German who denied democracy because its foundation was Christian: Karl Marx. He discovered that man spent much of his time earning a living. Universalizing this particular aspect, he gave us the economic man, for whom religion, culture, law, literature and the arts were by-products of his method of production. And thus did a German spawn Marxian Socialism.

Now we are at the beginning of a new fashion in men. With increases of taxes, decline in income, blind men discovered man lived in a State and was dependent on it for his ideas, his values, and thus was born the political man who has rights because the new lawyers told him the State gave him rights.

The partial views of man as expressed by Marx, Spencer, Darwin and Freud never treat man as he is—really is.

These views represent incidental activities erected into absolutes and are of much the same mental construction as would be shown by a dentist who thinks man is all teeth; or a manicurist who thinks he is all hands; or a pedicurist who thinks he is all feet; or a phrenologist who thinks he is all bumps.

Man, of course, is each of these things: he is biological; he is psychological; he is economic, and he is political, but he is none of these things exclusively nor is he all of these added together, any more than a baby is the sum of all the chemicals in a laboratory. We have taken man apart and looked at all the pieces, but like children with toys we cannot put him together again. In our fever for psycho-analysis, we have neglected psycho-synthesis.

Because the modern man is part-man, Christianity was watered down to suit these partial aspects. The result was that some did away with heaven and hell to suit economic man; some did away with sin and guilt, right and wrong to suit psychological man; others did away with theology and revelation to suit the Darwinian man; still others did away with the soul to suit political man and finally whittled away every trace of life until nothing was left.

The Christian view of man admits that man has ganglia, does dream, experiences libidos, works and talks politics, but it insists that man is exclusively none of these things. It begins by asking what is it that makes man different from anything else in the world; and answers an intellect and a will—an intellect by which he can know truth and a will by which he may choose goodness. Next, it says, since he is different from an animal he must have a different purpose than an animal, just as a monkey wrench must have a different purpose than a monkey. This purpose will obviously be in keeping with what is highest in his life, namely, an intellect and will. Man therefore wants Life—not for two more days, or two more months, but undying Life. He therefore wants Truth—not the truths of geography to the exclusion of science, nor of art to the exclusion of history, but all Truth without a mixture of error. He therefore wants Love, not love for a limited period of time, but an eternal ecstasy of Love without the shadow of hate or satiety. This Eternal Life, Truth, and Love for which he seeks is God. God therefore is his final and ultimate end. Therefore politics, economics, education, rationing, parliaments, parties, bureaucrats, governments, and social security are only means to that end and derive their morality from it. This is the foundation of the Christian order.

In order to understand man, one must begin with God, even more than to understand a sunbeam one must begin with the sun. God is the Creator of the world. He was not forced to create, any more than a poet is forced to write. He created freely out of the fullness of His Love. All good things diffuse themselves. Because the flower is good, it diffuses itself in perfume; because man is good, he gives; because God is good, He creates.

Among the creatures which He made, man was the peak of visible creation and for him all visible creation existed. This one creature He made free, in order that he might be capable of Love. No one can be forced to love; to be forced to love anyone is hell. Being made in His image and likeness, God intended that as man came from Love, so he should go back to Love after an earthly pilgrimage wherein he could freely say "Yea" or "Nay" to the courtship of the Divine Heart.

But in making man free, God made it possible for man to rebel. Man could be a traitor; he could be a soldier or he could be a deserter. Weighing all the possibilities, God chose to endow man with the power of rebellion in order that there might be meaning and purpose in allegiance, when he freely chose to give it.

In our language, God took the risk, and man, misinterpreting freedom as the right to do whatever he pleased, decided that he would be more free outside the law than within it. Instead of using creatures as a means to God, man decided to use them as an end and thus made gold, or the flesh, or power, the goal of living. He furthermore decided that instead of recognizing God as His Creator, he would make a Declaration of Independence and affirm himself as God. He thus committed the sin of lust by turning to creatures as an end, and the sin of pride by turning from God as his final end. Becoming hardened in his pride and lust, society became a confusion of conflicting self-centers instead of a fellowship of love which God intended it should be. The original freedom which was meant to be for God, and in God, became perverted to mean freedom from God.

This rebellion against God caused a fundamental disharmony inside man, for though he denies God, he still is God's creature. The prodigal son among the swine was still the son. Animals cannot rebel against their nature because they are not free, but man can rebel against his nature. He can deny his origin and his purpose, but he can never escape it. He could never lose the image in which he was created; he could never be free from his dependence on God. One can never be godless without God. Man could deface and mar the image but he could not destroy it; the great mosaics of Christ on the ceiling of the Saint Sophia in Constantinople were defaced by the Turks who could never succeed in destroying them. Man thus became a twisted distorted creature, wanting God because he was made in His image by Him and for Him, and yet hating God because man defaced that image. Destined for eternity, he has longings for eternal life and truth and love; but repudiating eternity, he tries to capture this life, and truth and love, where it is not—in the transitory fleeting shadow of time. Having lost the great gift of God's grace, he became not just a mere man but like a king in exile, dispossessed of a royalty and a stranger in a land that was meant to be a home.

That primal sin of human nature disturbed the equilibrium of human nature; as man rebelled against God, man rebelled against himself; his senses revolted against his reason; his flesh against his spirit; and even creatures seeing that their master had turned against God, now turned against their master. That is why there is not a one of us who does not feel that as St. Augustine put it, "Whatever we are, we are not what we ought to be."

This permanent wound in human nature cannot be explained away by biological evolution, as we tried to do a few years ago, because its essence is not the will to survive but pride which biology cannot touch. Selfishness is the root of the inexplicable tragedy of the world, namely: man's proud unwillingness to accept the absolute authority and the claim of God on Whose image he has been made. This is the mystery of iniquity! The optimism of the doctrine of Progress, that man becomes better and better as time goes on, cannot stand up under the facts of history which reveal increasing potentialities for chaos and war. Neither is there justification for the pessimism of Luther who said that man was intrinsically corrupt, nor for the pessimism of a Hobbes who said man was "solitary, poor, hasty, brutish and short." Man's sin did not make him utterly leprous and unclean, but it did impair his nature by breaking off relationship with Divine Love, darken his intellect and weaken his will, and make him personally more prone to sin.

The condition of regenerating a world is in recognizing the abysmal depths of evil in the heart of man, and realizing that public enemy No. 1 is neither ignorance, nor falls in evolution, nor bad government, nor ductless glands, but sin—apostasy from God.

This explains to some extent "how we got this way," but it is not the final word on the Christian doctrine of man.

God's love is limitless. As Love at the first moment of time could not keep the secrets of His Power and Goodness but told them to the nothingness in Creation, and later on could not keep the secrets of His Wisdom and told them to a chosen race in Revelation, so now Love completely surrenders Himself by appearing in the form and pattern of man as the person of Jesus Christ, true God and true man.

Man was made originally to the Image of God. Now that the image was defaced, who could better restore it than the Original Image according to which he was made? Thus the love that was spurned and rejected now appears in history as a Redeemer. The bridge between man and God had been broken down; only one who was both God and man could rebuild it. Being man, He could act as a man and for man; being God, His Redemption of man would have an infinite value.

Coming among sinful men, He allowed all their sins to come to a head and to do its worst against Him, namely put Him to death. Sin could do no more. But in attempting to kill God, which is the nature of sin, sin really wrote its own condemnation on the pages of history. For in rising from the dead by the power of God, He made the disaster of sin the beginning of its conquest, and the occasion of a new and regenerated humanity under His Headship which is the Kingdom of God.

If the Cross ended His life, if His Calvary was a hopeless fight against sin, then the pathos of our misery would be deepened and the riddle of our life darkened. But having met the enemy and overcome the worst, He becomes not only a Saviour but a final Authority who can tell us the way out of all the mad chaos of this hour. Thus we are confronted again with the original problem of Creation: the problem of "Either-Or." Either we will surrender our life and our will to Him and find peace, or we will repudiate Him wildly, completely and hatefully and end in cyclic wars. Either we will love Christ or we will love anti-Christ.

There is no more compulsion in this choice than in Creation. Man is still free. As in the beginning, he was free to accept God or reject Him, so now in history he is free to accept God's Son, Jesus Christ, or reject Him. The symbol of Christianity for that reason is the Cross, whereunto that Great Figure is nailed. Hands that are dug with steel cannot fashion a lash to break our wills. Feet that are pierced with nails cannot hunt us down as unwilling prey; lips that are bruised and parched can issue no dictatorial commands; eyes that are clotted and closed cannot make chains to enslave and imprison. His very flag is the flag of freedom, or better still the banner of love. He can only wait for us! But oh! How He waits: arms outstretched to embrace; heart open to love! No one else in all the world ever founded a religion wherein a welcome was extended to a sinner, while he was yet a sinner. But He does. "When as yet we were sinners. . . . Christ died for us" (Romans 5: 8, 9). All others are merely teachers: they tell us to wash ourselves righteous and then go to God. But He as a Saviour, bids us come dirty that He might have the joy of washing away our sins.

Everyone else demanded that we have a newness of life; He gives it, for there is no life apart from Him. Others make sin the condition of unacceptance; He makes sin the condition of acceptance: *O Felix Culpa.* "O Happy Fault that has won for us so loving, so mighty a Redeemer."

Such is the gesture of God's Mercy to fallen man. Instead of restoring man to what he had been, God did more. He stooped down from heaven, undoing the pride of Babel with the humility of Bethlehem, taking man unto His arms and drawing him to His Heart in an embrace so close that the gulf between the Creator and creature was bridged in a union as intimate as the branches and the vine.

Now contrast the modern pagan view of man. If this life is all why not get all we can and by whatever means we can? Why be faithful to one spouse if a more attractive one comes along? Why raise children and subject oneself to pain and confinement? Why be temperate and chaste and generous except in those moments which please us, or satiety overtakes us, or expediency demands it? Why should not the capitalist be greedy, the worker avaricious, the man on relief slothful? Why bother with distinctions between right and wrong, good and evil? Why not have a "progressive education" which would do away with restraint, discipline and authority? Why not substitute hygiene for morality? Why not make law the instrument of power? Why not be anti-Semitic, anti-Christian? Why not, as a well-known American journalist did, define freedom as the right to tell everyone who opposes our individual whims and fancies to go to hell?

A pagan who does none of these things is an inconsistent pagan, a cowardly pagan, a pagan half-afraid through Christian influence that he may be wrong. As G. K. Chesterton put it:

Now who that runs can read it,
The riddle that I write
Of why this poor old sinner
Should sin without delight?
But I, I cannot read it
(Although I run and run)
Of them that do not have the faith,
And will not have the fun.[1]

It is simply impossible to have millions of men in the world living according to their pagan principles, and not produce the modern chaotic world in which we live. This idea of a "Heaven here below" is the surest way to make a hell upon earth. The universe thus becomes a multiplicity of self-centered little deities; the coat of arms of each is a big letter "I," and when they talk their "I"'s are always getting closer together.

In the light of the foregoing explanation of man the choice before the world is this: Will we build a New Order on the totalitarian assumption that man is a tool of the State? Or will we retain the Old Order of the secularist culture of the last two hundred years, that man is only an economic animal? Or will we build a New Order on the Christian assumption, that man is a creature made to the image and likeness of God and therefore one for whom economics, politics, and society exist as a means to an eternal destiny beyond the historical perspective of planets, space, and time?

The post-war planners are still assuming with Marx that man is essentially economic, or with Darwin that he is essentially animal, or with Freud that he is essentially

---

[1] "The Song of the Strange Ascetic." From *The Collected Poems of G. K. Chesterton*. Copyright, 1911, by Dodd, Mead & Company, Inc.

sexual, or with Hitler that he is essentially political. Hence they think that all we have to do is to change an economic system, or form new parties, or give more sex instruction, or greater license to the break-up of the family and we will have peace.

These planners think they are practical, because they talk in terms of money, trade, international police and geo-graphical areas of influences and federated states. The truth is they are just as impractical as men who might leg-islate for squirrels by passing laws about nuts. Squirrels eat nuts, and man lives economically; but, as nuts do not ex-plain squirrels, so neither does production explain man. Because the planners do not understand the nature of the one for whom they are planning, their plans are going to lead us into a phase of history where ". . . eldest Night and Chaos, Ancestors of Nature, hold Eternal Anarchy, amidst the voice of Endless Wars."[2]

Given the errant impulses, the frustrated selfish exis-tences, the distorted human goals which these partial views of man engender, there is only one way to arrest that chaos, and that is by organizing it, and the organization of chaos is Socialism. The individualism and egotism which a dis-torted concept of man begets leave him alone and isolated, and to overcome this isolation there is only one non-Christian solution possible: the sub-ordination of these rebellious atoms to a compulsory principle in the hands of the State. Socialism is the secularized, atheized version of a community and a fraternity of man which Christian love alone can engender. It is the new form into which man will bring his tortured and isolated personality, in vain quest for peace. By abusing his freedom under Liberalism, man,

---

[2] Milton, *Paradise Lost*, Book II.

unless he returns to a knowledge of his true nature, will fall under the compulsion of Socialism. He will think less and less of freedom, though he may talk much about it, for a man talks about his health when he is unhealthy. His end will be the trading of his freedom for a false security from the wet-nurse of the State.

The old order of Liberal Individualism is dead. Man will either become the subject of a non-divine evil will embodied in socialistic bureaucracy, or he will submit himself to the higher Divine Principle for Whom he was made and in Whom he alone can find his peace. He no longer will be free to decide whether he will or will not live under authority. From now on it is a question of under whose authority he will live, the authority of a socialistic State, or the authority of God reflected in a State which recognizes each person as endowed with rights and possessed of a value which no power can disinherit.

The Western World must learn that Totalitarianism cannot be overcome by Socialism, by laissez-faire Capitalism, by Individualism, or by any combination of these, for what has gone wrong is not the means of living, but the ends. The economic and political chaos of the modern world can be overcome only by a non-political non-economic, non-Marxian, non-Freudian concept of a man and society. This does not mean that politics and economics are of no value; they are. But it means they are of secondary value for, unless we know the nature of the creature for whom politics and economics exist, it is just as useless to meddle with them as it is to fool with a blast furnace unless we know its purpose. Unless we restore the Christian concept of man, and thus build a human rather than an economic order, we will be forced into a Totalitarianism in the hour we are doing our most to combat it.

What is the objection to the basic Christian principle, that we build for the whole man as a creature of God instead of for the Darwinian, Freudian, Marxian man? The answer is on the tongues of all the reactionaries: "Christianity does not suit the modern man." Certainly it does not. And for the reason that the modern man is not man; he is part-man, a dissected man.

But Christianity does however suit man in his entirety, or human nature as it is, composed of body and soul and made to the image and likeness of God, with horizontal relations to the right and left in space and time, and yet never wholly explained by these, because identified with something prior and more fundamental, namely vertical relations with God, His Creator and Redeemer in Whom is his Peace and his Joy.

Until now it has been said Christianity does not suit the modern man, therefore scrap Christianity. Now let us say, Christianity does not suit modern man, therefore let us scrap modern man.

Maybe there is nothing wrong with Christianity after all; maybe—may we dare suggest it—there is something wrong with us. Maybe there is something wrong with John Dewey and nothing wrong with St. John; maybe there is something false about H. G. Wells, and nothing wrong with Vincent de Paul; maybe there is something wrong with Gertrude Stein, and something right about St. Gertrude; maybe there is something wrong with Progressive Education and nothing wrong with the Light of the World Who said: "Suffer the little children to come unto me." Maybe science cannot be a substitute for morality; maybe morality is not identical with self-will; maybe the goal of life is not to get seven per cent on mortgages; maybe the goal of economics is not for management to be responsible to bondholders, but to be responsible to the common good; maybe self-expression raised to a national form could end in Nazism; maybe we have been wrong. Maybe, we had better get back to God! We have given the Darwinians their chance; we have given the Marxists their chance; we have given the Freudians their chance; we have given the Hitlerites their chance. Now, let us give man a chance.

CHAPTER FIVE

Man's Christian Character

Why have not the moral forces of a nation, such as education, the press, radio, the clergy and social reformers been more insistent on developing a new order instead of patching up an old one? Perhaps the principal reason is because they have been getting behind certain movements instead of ahead of them. The first thought that comes to a particular group who wishes to further legislation in their favour, is to wire educators, clergymen and actors and social workers to sign their names sponsoring their cause. There are at least five hundred such professional signers in our country who keep their fountain pens uncapped for such cheap publicity. It is just this irrational mentality, which substitutes imitations for thinking and which pushes some group or class instead of leading the common good, that has paralyzed the regeneration of society.

A few generations ago it was a fashion to get behind Capitalism as political parties were formed to support their legislation. Now it is the fashion and mood to get behind

Labour which develops its own parties, while the common good is ignored. Each class demands its rights in the name of freedom, forgetting that as Lincoln once said: "Sheep and wolves never agree on the definition of freedom."

The Christian solution is to be neither behind Capital nor Labour exclusively, but to be behind Capital when Marxian Socialism would destroy private property, to be behind Labour when Monopolistic Capitalism would claim the priority of profits over the right to a comfortable wage, and to be behind the common good when either Capital or Labour would injure it.

If we are behind either Capital or Labour, at what point will either stop in their demands? Or is there a stopping point? Did Capital ever decide for itself when it was in the saddle that it would take no more than ten per cent profits? Capital took all the profits the traffic would bear. Now that Capital is unseated and Labour is riding the economic horse, what limits does Labour set itself? Is there a wage beyond which it will not ask? Are there certain minimum hours below which it will not work? They too will get all the traffic will bear. When self-interest and class interest become the standard, then who shall say there is a right and wrong? As the old Chinese proverb put it: "No good rat will injure the grain near its hole."

This brings us to a consideration of the economic and political principle of the Christian order. The Christian order starts with man; all other orders start with a class. Capitalism and Communism, for example, though opposite in their directions, like branches of a tree, are nevertheless rooted in the same economic principle that a class takes all. Communism is only rotted Capitalism. Under Capitalism the employer takes all; under Communism the worker takes all.

The basic principle of the Christian order is this: economic activity is not the end of life, but the servant of human life. Therefore, the true primary end of economic production is not profit but the satisfaction of human needs. The old order was: consumption exists for production, and production for finance. The Christian order reverses it: finance exists for production, and production for consumption. This demands a revolutionary change of the whole economic order because it affirms the primacy of the human over the economic. Its starting principle is that the right of a man to a living wage is prior to the right of returns on investments.

From this basic principle the Christian Economic Character draws the following conclusions: when an industry cannot pay a wage sufficient not only for a moderately comfortable life but also for savings, the difference should be made up either by industry pooling a percentage of all wages paid, or in default of this, by the State.

Neither the capitalists' right to profits nor the labourers' right to organization are absolute and unlimited; they are both subjected to the common good of all. Both the right to profits and the right to organization are means, and as a means they are to be judged by the way they promote the true ends of life: religion, general prosperity, peace, and happy human relations. These rights therefore can be suspended for the common good of all.

The consumer must not be treated as the indispensable condition of unlimited demands by Labour or unlimited profits by Capital, but as the person whose interest is the true end of the whole process.

The distinction between Capital and Labour, which is based on whether one buys labour or sells it, must be broken down. It must give way to a union of Capital and

Labour on the basis of the common service they render
to the nation. To ask which is more important, Capital or
Labour, is like asking which is more important to a man,
the right leg or the left. Since they both have a common
function, they should function together. Conflicts between
Capital and Labour are wrong, not because they hold up
the delivery of goods, but for the moral reason that they
create distorted personal relationships, as the quarrel of a
husband and wife disrupts the good of the family.

The wage contract whenever possible should be mod-
ified somewhat by a contract of partnership between
employer and employee so that the wage earners are made
sharers in some sort in the profits, management or ownership of industry. Since both produce a social wealth there
is no reason why both should not share in the wealth produced. A worker in a factory has more right to the profits
of his industry than a man who clips coupons. The only
way to make labour responsible is to give it some capital
to defend; and the only way to make capital responsible
is to make it labour for its right to possess it. Did anyone
ever hear of an artist agitating for a seven-hour day? Why
not? Because his work is his life. Today men do not work;
they have employment. Work is a divine vocation; employment is an economic necessity. A labourer will sit down on
someone else's tools, but no artist will sit down on his paint
brushes. The reason is that the artist's work entails responsibility. That is why those who are exclusively getting
behind either Capitalists to defend them against Labour
racketeers, or behind Labour to defend them against economic royalists, are delaying the day of economic peace
and contributing to a future economic conflict which the
Communists seek to thrust upon this country. The Christian solution is to unite them on a basis of a common task.

Political Charter

The primary end of political and social life is the conservation, the development, and the perfection of the human person as a creature made to the image and likeness of God. Hence the State exists for man, not man for the State.

The political and social activity of the State is directed primarily not to any one class, or party or race or group, but to the common good of all, by creating those external conditions which are needed for the material, intellectual and religious development of man.

The State, in the just fulfilment of its rights and in the exercise of its authority, will always recognize its responsibility to the Eternal Judge before whose Tribunal every wrong judgment and every revolt against morality will receive one day its just retribution and judgment.

The State while justly altering an acquisitive society which made profits primary to the human, must avoid falling into the opposite extreme of substituting for the acquisitiveness of money an acquisitiveness of power.

Democracy should be extended, not curtailed. For many decades political power was controlled to a great extent by organized Capital, by merchants, lords of finance, and industrialists. Today the stage is being prepared for the control of political power by Labour. A class transmission of power is opposed to the basic principles of democracy. The Christian concept of politics is that government exists for the common good of all. If democracy is to be made effective the holders of economic power whomsoever they be must be made responsible to the community. They are its servants, not its masters. There once was a day when Capital appealed to government to protect it; now Labour appeals to government to protect it, and the only bond which unites them is their unconscious opposition to the common good.

The Christian would seek the broadening of democracy. Presently there is Political Democracy with a representation based on geography, that is, on population and on States which constitute the House and the Senate, which must be continued. But why should there not be Industrial Democracy wherein there will be not only a geographical but vocational representation, namely one based on the work citizens contribute to the general welfare. There are already a number of natural bonds existing between employees and employer, for example, those who engage in mining, transportation, communication, building, etc. The railroaders, even though they be separated, talk a common language because they have a common task. Men are more naturally united on the basis of their work than on the basis of their Congressional District. This is not saying that the present methods of representation should be abandoned. They should not. It is only saying that democracy should be extended to recognize these vocational groups. No citizen ever enthuses about meeting a fellow citizen from the same Congressional District, but a railroad man from San Francisco and a railroad man from New York have common interests. Why should there not be a recognition of these various unions or organizations; and when we speak of unions, we mean here employers and employees, within the same vocational group.

At the present time men are bound together according to the position they occupy in the labour market, that is, whether they buy labour or whether they sell it, which is the basis of the conflict of Capital and Labour. This opposition can be done away with by recognizing groups on the basis of the diverse functions they exercise in society. Just as men who live near one another naturally unite themselves into municipalities, so too those who practice the same trade, or profession, economic or otherwise, should form vocational groups.

When America was a young country, representation on the basis of individuals was sufficient; but now it has grown together like a body. It is no longer composed of individuals or cells; it has spontaneously formed natural unities. The body grows from individual cells and forms organs, for example, heart, lungs, cells which mediate between the cells and the head. Our nation has grown into such a network of relationships, associations and fellowships. It is in these that the real wealth of our nation consists. Why should not these industrial units, made up of the employers and the employees in the same profession or vocation be recognized? Who has more to do with the common good, in a material way, than they? And would not their recognition by government do away with pressure groups in our legislation? The way to make democracy work is to make it democratic.

Representative democracy is today based on hardly anything more than mechanical divisions of geography and population. The result being that there is too great a gap between the work performed by citizens and the contribution of that work to the nation as a whole. Too many citizens feel their vote means little; they have no consciousness of being politically represented, since the primary earthly interests of a man are his occupation and his livelihood.

The reason the existence of these groups is ignored is because we have not been thinking on Christian principles, but rather on the principles of Rationalism, which thought of everything as being either particular or universal. Hence we had first a society based on Individualism, and now in some parts of the world a society based on Collectivism, as if there were no alternative. There is an alternative in the human body, between the head and the cells, *viz.:* the organs. There is also an alternative in political life, namely this network of social relationships, based on the common task of employers and employees in a common calling.

The great revolutions which have swept the world since the first World War were in their higher reaches, strivings for fellowship—Communism basing it on the class, Fascism on corporations and Nazism on race or blood. All three were wrong because they were too exclusive, because they derived their unity from a dictator, instead of from themselves—and because they liquidated all opposition, *e.g.* kulaks, Italian liberals, and Jews. The national craving of man for fellowship and unity, America can supply on democratic principles, *i.e.* on the basis of a common service to a common cause. The nation would then be made up of a series of unities. A member of each particular group, for example, mining, farming, dairying will do all that he can for his own group while recognizing that the self-interest of his own group will be subject to the greater interest of the nation of which he is a part.

One of the greatest enemies of Democracy is a Fascism which refuses to recognize that these employer-employee units have arisen spontaneously in society. Fascism imposes leadership on such associations from above. Democracy, on the contrary, insists that being natural associations they should choose their own leadership. No dictator at the top of the pile shall organize or lead them; they organize and lead themselves.

A nation will then be made up of circles of loyalties. Just as a member of a family has a duty to submerge his individual assertiveness for the good of the family, so too these natural associations of men will have their present self-assertiveness merged by recognizing the prior claim of the nation. The nation would then be not only a union of states, which it must remain, but also a community of communities, each community of which is free to guide its own activities, provided it falls within the general order of communal life and does not injure the freedom of other communities.

In other words, the Christian principle in the economic and political order seeks to end the conflict between Capital and Labour by making them co-partners in a common responsibility. The principle will not be, "What do I get out of this?" but "What service can I render to my country?" Freedom, fellowship, service, these are the principles of a Christian social order, derived from the basic principle that man is a creature of God, destined after a life of free service to enjoy eternal fellowship with Divine Love.

In order to build up a new world, we must begin thinking in a new way. Just as Totalitarianism cannot be defeated by thinking down the same roads which led to it, so neither can the selfishness, the egoism, and the class-conflicts of our social order be conquered by patching up the principles which produced it.

We must re-think on the Christian principle that production exists primarily for consumption. The old Liberal principle that workers are "hands," must give way to the Christian principle that workers are "persons," and therefore may never be permitted to sink below the human level. The old Liberal principle that finance may determine production must give way to the Christian principle, that the hungry and the needy and the common good must determine production. The old Liberal idea that culture is a product of economics, must give way to the Christian idea that economics is a by-product of culture, and that unless our morals are right our economics will be wrong. The old Liberal idea which recognized only the individual and the State must give way to the Christian idea which recognizes intermediate groupings, in each of which a man can feel that he counts for something, and that others depend on him, and he on them. The old Liberal idea that the State is only a policeman protecting property must give way to the Christian idea that the State is a Moral Person, protecting persons and communities of persons. The old Liberal idea that representation is limited to individuals in geographical areas must be supplemented by the Christian idea that representation must include the various groupings of men on the basis of the service they render to the nation. The old Liberal idea that freedom is to be used for self-interest must give way to the Christian idea that freedom is justified only when it expresses itself in fellowship, as the eye is free to see only when it functions within the body and not outside it. The old Liberal idea that Democracy is political must be supplemented by the Christian idea that it is also economic, and that just as men have something to say about the country where they vote, so they shall have something to say about the place where they work.

Why is it so important that we start with an entirely new set of principles, and a new standard of values? Because, if we do not, we will end only by shifting power and booty from one party and class to another, instead of working for the good of all.

This war is the end of the Economic Man, and by the Economic Man is meant the Man whose basic principle was the primacy of profit. Unless we accept Christian principles based on the Primacy of the Person and the common good, we will end in the enthronement of Political Man. This is where the irreligious revolutions of both Marxian

Socialism and Nazism ended: in the substitution of the acquisitiveness of power for the acquisitiveness of money. And the Political Man whose god is power can be just as lustful, just as avaricious, as the Economic Man whose god is money. The decent human person has little to choose between the two.

Either we will restore Christian order based on the dignity of the human person, or we will shift from a régime dictated by economics to one dictated by politics. This is the tendency in world politics as the State shifts from its original basis of popular sovereignty to a totalitarian basis in which the State is an end in itself.

There are four steps upwards to the modern socialistic State. The first was the false principle of the sixteenth century that the religion of the State was the religion of its prince, by which national churches were substituted for a Catholic or universal Church. The second step was the Age of Reason in which the State became secularized by divorcing politics from ethics, and economics from morality. The third step was Marxian Socialism in which the Church was liquidated by the State. And the fourth step is Nazism where the State is substituted for the Church.

Nothing so proves an utter and absolute ignorance of the facts of history than to be fearful of the union of the Church and the State. Rather all the facts point to the danger of the State absorbing the Church. It was Christ who said: "Render to Cæsar the things that are Cæsar's." It is the new State which says: "Render to Cæsar the things that are God's."

The Omnipotent State of Political Man has only one enemy, the Church. It knows it cannot absorb man totally, until it suppresses the Church which says that the soul belongs to God. That is why it persecutes the Church.

Education is incapable of stopping the Omnipotent State because education will belong to the State. Einstein is our witness that when political power substituted itself for economic power, the universities and the schools failed because they were already part of that world. Only the Church defended man. He said: "Being a lover of freedom, when the revolution came in Germany, I looked to the universities to defend it, knowing that they had always boasted of their devotion to the cause of truth; but no, the universities immediately were silenced. Then I looked to the great editors of the newspapers whose flaming editorials in days gone by had proclaimed their love of freedom; but they, like the universities, were silenced in a few short weeks. . . .

"Only the Church stood squarely across the path of Hitler's campaign for suppressing truth. I never had any special interest in the Church before, but now I feel a great affection and admiration because the Church alone has had the courage and persistence to stand for intellectual truth and moral freedom. I am forced thus to confess that what I once despised I now praise unreservedly."

This war is an expression of a world disease. It will avail us naught to give this old order artificial respiration, for we are doing it to a corpse. Let us wear no widow's weeds of mourning because our superstitions are being carried to the grave. Rather should we be putting on our wedding garments to court a new world and a new order, in a renewed Divine Justice.

If the old world of politicians who promise to the electorate everything it wants, from pillaging the Treasury to new tyres and more sugar, is passing,

If the old world of Capitalism, which thinks that property rights mean the right to accumulate profits uncontrolled by the common good and the rights of organized labour is dead,

If the old world of labour organizations which thinks there is no minimum to hours of work, and no maximum to salary demands, and which would paralyze a national industry for five days, because of a five-cent transportation charge, is dead,

If the old world where a college education was a social necessity, instead of being what it ought to be—an intellectual privilege—is dead,

If the old world of social Christianity which emptied religion of God, and Christianity of Christ, and which thought the whole business of religion was to drive an ambulance for social workers or to pipe naturalistic tunes for the intelligentsia who said they were only animals, is dead,

Let it perish!

We are a creative people; we are responsive to human rights and needs as no nation in the world is responsive; we have tremendous powers of renewal. We must not delay the reconstruction, for when the boys come home from the battlefronts of the world they will share none of the old ideas. Every one of them will want a job and they will have a right to one, whether they belong to a union or not; they will not admit that joining a union is the only condition on which a man may work. Every one of them will want a living wage and the right to raise a family in comfort and decency, and they will not admit that these personal and family rights are subject to and conditioned upon bond-holders receiving six per cent interest on their investments. Every one of them will have lived through a day when Capital ruled and when Labour ruled; and because they fought for neither, while at war, they will fight for neither in peace. But they will fill up a great vacuum in our economic and political life, as they fight for the Common Good in which the uncommon man of Capital and the common man of organized power will both be subject to the resurrection of a Justice under God. And with God on their side—who can stand against them!

CHAPTER SIX

Conspiracy Against Life

The Christian order demands the restoration of those areas of life which are life-growing, life-sustaining, and life-forwarding, *viz.:* the family. As from the impoverishment of cells in the body there flows the tragedy of death, so from the disintegration of the family there springs and spreads the dry-rot of the body-politic, the nation and the world. As the family is the school of sacrifice wherein we first learn to bear each other's burdens, so the decay of the family is the unlearning of those sacrifices which bring on the decay of a nation as it faces the miseries and horrors of life.

That the family is disintegrating in our national life, no one will deny. The modern husband and wife, like isolated atoms, resent the suggestion that they should lose their identity in the family molecule. It is each for himself as against all for one and one for all. And when there is an offspring, never before have children been so distant and so separated from their parents. The family hardly ever meets. The family that once had permanent headquarters, now has none, as the mother assumes she contributes more to the nation by making bullets than by raising babies. About the only time the family meets is after midnight, when the home becomes a hotel, and the more money they have the less they meet. Less time is passed together than is spent at a motion picture, or a beauty parlour. Courtship takes place outside the home, generally in a crowded room with a low ceiling, amidst suffocating smoke, while listening to a tom-tom orchestra glamoured by a girl who invariably cannot sing. The wife listens to radio serials with their moans, groans and commercials, wherein triangles are more common than in a geometry book. She reads magazine articles by women who never stay at home, saying that a woman's place is in the home. The family Bible recording dates of birth and baptism is no longer existent because few read the Bible, few give birth, and few are ever baptised. The intelligentsia love to read George Bernard Shaw on the family: "Unless woman repudiates her womanliness, her duty to her husband, to her children, to everyone but herself, she cannot emancipate herself." And as for Catholics there is hardly a Catholic man or woman in the United States today over fifty years of age who cannot remember that in the days of his or her youth the rosary was said every evening in the family circle and everyone was there. How many do it now?

The two most evident symptoms of the breakdown of the family are: divorce and voluntary or deliberate sterility, *i.e.* broken contracts and frustrated loves. Divorce destroys the stability of the family; voluntary sterility destroys its continuity. Divorce makes the right of living souls hang up the caprice of the senses and the terminable pact of selfish fancy; while voluntary sterility makes a covenant with death, extracting from love its most ephemeral gift while disclaiming all its responsibilities. It is a great conspiracy against life in which science, which should minister to life, is used as it is in war—to frustrate and destroy; it is a selfishness which is directed neither to saving nor to earning, but only to spending; it is an egotism, which because it admits of no self-control, seeks to control even the gifts of God; it sees sex not as something to solder life, but to scorch the flesh; it is a denial that life is a loan from the great bank of life and must be paid back again with the interest of life, and not with death.

It is a world wherein musicians are always picking up their bows and violins, but never making music; a world wherein chisel is touched to marble, but a statue is never created; a world where brush is lifted to canvas, but a portrait is never born; a world wherein talents are buried in a napkin as life plays recreant to its sacred messiahship. It is therefore a world wherein the thirst for love is never satisfied for never will they who break the lute snare the music.

We as Christians have argued with those who believe in divorce and the mechanical frustration of love, but our arguments convinced no one. Not because the arguments were not sound. That is the trouble. They are too good! Good reasons are powerless against emotions. Like two women arguing over back fences, we are arguing from different premises. The majority of people who are opposed to the stability and continuity of family life, for the most part do not believe in the moral law of God. They may say they believe in God, but it is not the God of Justice. Few believe in a future life, entailing Divine Judgment, with the possible sanction of eternal punishment. Even professed Christians among them when confronted with the text: "What therefore God hath joined together, let no man put asunder" (Mark 10: 9), will retort that God never intended that it should be so.

They argue from the need of pleasure, the necessity of avoiding sacrifice, and the primacy of the economic. We argue from the Eternal Reason of God rooted in nature, the teachings of His Incarnate Son, Jesus Christ the Redeemer of the world.

There is absolutely no common denominator between us. It is like trying to convince a blind man that there are seven colours in a spectrum, or like arguing with a snob that a ditch-digger is his equal.

Instead then of arguing against the modern pagan who believes in the disruption of the family, let us assume that his premises are right, namely, man is only an animal; that morality is self-interest; that if there is a God, He never intended that we should not do as we please, that every individual is his own standard of right and wrong; that the amount of wealth one has must be the determinant of the incarnations of mutual love; that when we die that is the end of us, or if there be a heaven we all go there independently of how we conduct ourselves in life.

Now, once you start with these principles, then certainly divorces are right; then certainly avoid children; then certainly shirk sacrifices. If we are only beasts, and love is sex, then there is no reason why anyone should assume responsibility.

But why not go all the way? By the same principle anything is right if I can get away with it. If the bonds between husband and wife are revocable at will and for the advantage of self-love, why should not the treaties between nation and nation be revocable at the will of either partner? If a husband may steal the wife of another man, why should not Germany steal Poland? If the possession of a series of lust-satisfying partners is the right of man, why should not the possession of a series of slave colonies be the right of a nation? If John Smith can break his treaty to take Mary Jones until death, who shall say Italy is wrong in breaking its treaties with Ethiopia, or that Japan is wrong in seizing Manchuria? If this life is all, if there is no Moral Order dependent on God, then any man is a fool for being true to his contract.

Why not do away with all business credit? Why should the government pay us for the bonds we buy? Why should we not repudiate our loyalty and trust? What guarantee have we of credit, when the most vital of all compacts can be "sworn" with reservations? Why should not international treaties be like marriage treaties: "not worth the paper they are written on?"

If divorces from marital contracts, why not divorces from international contracts? If in domestic society moderns sneer at marital fidelity as "bourgeois virtue," what right have they to ask that "bourgeois virtue" should be recognized in world society? "If the trumpet give forth an uncertain sound who shall prepare for battle?"

If the economic is primary to the human, then why should not the capitalist be more interested in profits, than in the right of subsistence of his workers; then why not artificially limit children for the sake of the economic and the financial? If a man outgrows his clothes why should he not starve himself; if he lacks bread, why should he not pull out his teeth; if there is not enough room on a ship, why not like mutineers at sea throw sleeping comrades to the sharks? In each case it is the same principle: the primacy of the economic over the human.

We are at war with Hitler because he makes the human secondary to the racial. What is so different to making the human secondary to the economic? If Marxist Socialism says that only those belonging to a certain class shall live, and Fascism that only those belonging to a certain nation shall live, and, if we say that only those who have a certain bank account shall live or have the right to live, we are emptying our cause of all morality. Universalize this principle and in the end no one will be permitted to play a piano unless he does it in a grand salon, nor shall anyone have the right to drink cocktails unless he is in evening clothes. Such snobbishness is anti-democratic. It is wicked, because it exalts the economic over the human.

Some time ago a Nazi soldier in occupied France took his French wife into a hospital. Seeing a crucifix on the wall, he ordered the nun to take it down. She refused! He ordered her again saying that he did not want his child ever to look upon the image of a crucified Jew. The nun took it down under threats. The father's wish was fulfilled to the letter. The child was born—blind. Now shall we say only those of an economic status have the right to bring children into the world, as the Nazi said that only those of a certain race had a right?

And so we go back to the beginning. If we are only animals and not moral creatures of God, then certainly act like animals; then certainly permit divorces, and a pharmacopoeia of devices, prophylactic and eugenic, to cultivate the animal that man is; make it a universe where the ethics of man are no different from the ethics of the barnyard and the stud.

Some day because of the refusal to live for others, to the full extent of our capacity, there will be the haunting conscience. As John Davidson puts it:

> Your cruellest pain is when you think of all
> The honied treasure of your bodies spent
> And no new life to show. O then you feel
> How people lift their hands against themselves,
> And taste the bitterest of the punishment
> Of those whom pleasure isolates. Sometimes
> When darkness, silence, and the sleeping world
> Give vision scope, you lie awake and see
> The pale sad faces of the little ones
> Who should have been your children, as they press
> Their cheeks against your windows, looking in
> With piteous wonder, homeless, famished babes,
> Denied your wombs and bosoms.[1]

In contrast to this pagan view of life, the Christian principles governing the family are these:

Marriage, naturally and supernaturally, is one, un-breakable unto death: Naturally, because there are only two words in the vocabulary of love: "You" and "Always." "You," because love is unique; "Always," because love is eternal. Supernaturally, because the union of husband and wife is modeled upon the union of Christ and His Church, which endures through the agelessness of eternity.

The foundation of marriage is love, not sex. Sex is phys-iological and of the body: love is spiritual and therefore of the will. Since the contract is rooted not in the emotions, but in the will, it follows that when the emotion ceases, the contract is not dissolvable, for the love of the will is not subject to the vicissitudes of passion. A lifetime is not too long for two beings to become acquainted with each other, for marriage should be a series of perpetual and successive

---

[1] *"Testament of John Davidson."*

revelations, the sounding of new depths, and the manifestation of new mysteries. At one time, it is the mystery of the other's incompleteness which can be known but once, because capable of being completed but once; at another time, the mystery is of the other's mind; at another the mystery is of fatherhood and motherhood which before never existed; and finally there is mystery of being shepherds for little sheep ushering them into the Christ Who is the door of the sheepfold.

Love by its nature is not exclusively mutual self-giving, otherwise love would end in mutual exhaustion, consuming its own useless fire. Rather it is mutual self-giving which ends in self-recovery. As in heaven, the mutual love of a Father for Son recovers itself in the Holy Ghost, the Bond of Unity, so too the mutual love of spouse for spouse recovers itself in the child who is the incarnation of their lasting affection. All love ends in an Incarnation, even God's.

Procreation then is not in imitation of the beasts of the field, but of the Divine God where the love that vies to give is eternally defeated in the love that receives and perpetuates. All earthly love therefore is but a spark caught from the Eternal Flame of God.

Every child is a potential nobleman for the Kingdom of God. Parents are to take that living store from the quarry of humanity, cut and chisel it by loving discipline, sacrifice, mould it on the pattern of the Christ-Truth until it becomes a fit stone for the Temple of God, whose architect is Love. To watch a garden grow from day to day, especially if one has dropped the seed himself and cared for it, deepens the joy of living. But it is nothing compared to the joy of watching other eyes grow, conscious of another image in their depths.

At a time when the first wild ecstasies begin to fade, when the husband might be tempted to believe that another woman is more beautiful than his wife, and the wife might be tempted to believe that another husband would be more chivalrous—it is at that moment that God in His Providence sends children. Then it is, that in each boy, the wife sees the husband reborn in all his chivalry and promises; and in each girl, the husband sees his wife reborn in all her sweetness and beauty. The natural impulse of pride that comes with begetting, the new love that overblooms the memory of a mother's pain as she swings open the portals of flesh, and the joy of linked creatures in each other's fruit, are as so many links in the rosary of love binding them together in an ineffable and unbreakable union of love. Deliberately frustrate these incarnations of mutual love and you weaken the tie, as love dies by its own "too much."

Since nature has associated private property in a very special manner with the existence and development of the family, it follows that the State should diffuse private property through the family that its functions may be preserved and perfected.

If the bringing of children into the world is today an economic burden, it is because the social system is inadequate; and not because God's law is wrong. Therefore the State should remove the causes of that burden. The human must not be limited and controlled to fit the economic, but the economic must be expanded to fit the human.

Since the family by nature is prior to the State, and more sacred than the State, it is the duty of the State to establish such internal conditions of life as will not hamper a Christian home life.

The head of the family should be paid a wage sufficient for the family and which will make possible an assured, even if modest, acquisition of private property.

The State should defend the indissolubility of the marriage ties rather than weaken the sanctity of contracts, for divorces are in the highest degree hostile to the prosperity of families and of States, springing as they do from the depraved morals of the people.

Such is the Christian position concerning marriage, and one that is, outside the Church, almost universally misunderstood. It is so often said: "They can divorce and remarry, because they are not Catholics," or "the Catholic Church says that deliberate frustration of the fruits of love is wrong." No! No! No! Divorce and voluntary sterility are not wrong because the Church says they are wrong. Why does the Church say they are wrong? The Church says they are wrong because they are violations of the natural law, which binds all men. There is not one God for Catholics and another God for Hottentots. And all who violate the natural law will be punished by God. A modern pagan is no more free to break God's law than a Catholic.

But why does almost everyone outside of the Church associate the objection to divorce and voluntary sterility with the Church? Because the Church is today alone defending the natural law. If a time ever came when the Church alone defended that natural truth that two and two make four, the world would say: "It is a Catholic doctrine." As the natural law continues to be defended only by the Church, a day will come when Catholics will have to be prepared to die for the truth that it is wrong to poison mothers-in-law and that apples are green in the springtime.

Sometimes nations and people learn through experience that a violation of the natural law is wrong. Such expressions as "crime does not pay," or "you cannot get away with it," or "it pays to live right," mean that, having burned our fingers, we learn that it is in obedience to law, and not in rebellion against it, that we find peace. No country better illustrates this than Russia. In the first flush of its atheistic Marxian Socialism, it denied the necessity of marriage, established abortion centers, ridiculed fidelity and chastity as a "bourgeois virtue," compared lust and adultery to drinking a glass of water, after which you could forget the glass in one instance, and the person in the other; introduced postcard divorces, which required only that you send a notice that you were no longer living with a certain party, and all obligations thereby ceased.

Now, like a man who violates the natural law by over-drinking and then learns to respect the law through ruined health, so too Russia, by violating the natural law of marriage, has learned through its tragic effects to respect it. In 1934, without even cracking a smile, the Russians repudiated their Communistic immorality by a complete somersault, as the government declared "divorces and remarriage were a petty bourgeois deviation from Communist ideals." Divorces were made more difficult; fees for divorces were increased, so that, "silly girls would think twice before marrying a man with twenty or thirty records." Postcard divorces were abolished. Frequent remarriage after divorce was legally identified with rape and punished as such. Abortion clinics were eliminated; desertion was considered "bourgeois." On November 29, 1941, a tax was imposed on single persons and childless married couples, and a Decree of June 27, 1936, which sought to increase the size of the family, set up a system of payment to parents on the basis of the number of their children. Premiums were paid to mothers for every child after the sixth, and payments increased with the eleventh and subsequent children. Under this law a billion and a quarter

million roubles were paid out by the government in the first
nine months of 1941.

In 1919, Russia regarded the Christian concept of purity, chastity, and marriage with its unbreakable union, its
forbidding of divorce and deliberate control of the number
of children in a family, abortion and the like, as "bourgeois
virtues." But the Russia of today we find looking on divorce,
voluntary sterility, desertion, abortion, and the breakdown
of family life as "bourgeois vices." Such change reveals not
only the inner inconsistency of Marxian Socialism, but
more than that, how Russia has apparently learned something that we in America have not yet learned, namely, that
you cannot build a strong nation by disintegrating the family. It is conceivable that, in this respect, Russian family life
may stand higher in the eyes of God, than America's.

If some of our "pinks," intelligentsia, fellow travellers,
and Reds, who are under orders to bore into Civilian Defence to disrupt this country, would keep up-to-date, they
might learn that they are trying to impose upon America
the very scum which Russia rejected. History testifies that
the prosperity of the State and the temporal happiness of
its citizens cannot remain safe and sound where the foundation on which they are established, namely, the moral
order, is weakened and where the very fountainhead from
which the State draws its life, namely, wedlock and the
family, is obstructed by the vices of its citizens.

A downward step in the stability of the family was
taken on December 21, 1942, when the Supreme Court
of the United States held that a divorce granted in Nevada
must be accepted by every other state. There were only two
dissenting votes, one by Mr. Justice Murphy, the other by
Mr. Justice Jackson. The latter wrote the dissenting opinion, calling the Court's decision "demoralizing."

A few of his many objections against the majority opinion may be cited: (*a*) "The Court's decision . . . nullifies the power of each state to protect its own citizens against the dissolution of their marriages by other states." (*b*) "To declare that a state is powerless to protect either its own policy or the family rights of its people . . . repeals the divorce laws of all the states and substitutes the law of Nevada to all marriages, one of the parties of which can afford a short trip there." (*c*) "Settled family relationships may be destroyed by a procedure that we would not recognize if the suit were one to collect a grocery bill."

The universalizing of easy divorce means that the institution of marriage is slowly degenerating into State-licensed free love.

Legalized polygamy and polyandry are recognized now on condition that husbands or wives, as the case may be, do not harness other wives or husbands together to the coach of their egotism, but that they hitch them up in tandem fashion, or single file. To the extent that the courts disrupt this natural unity of a nation, they will incapacitate themselves for international fellowship. For if we destroy this inner circle of loyalty through disloyalty, how shall we build up the larger international circles of loyalty from which world peace is derived?

Without realizing it we may be getting back to a condition which shocked Cæsar. Plutarch tells us that one day Julius Cæsar saw some wealthy foreign women in Rome carrying dogs in their arms and he said: "Do the women in their country never bear children?" Apparently, even in those days, maternal instincts which should have been directed to children were perverted, in certain cases, to pomeranians.

Men and women of America, raise altars to Life and Love while there is time! If the citadel of married happiness has not been found it is because some have failed to lay siege to the outer walls of their own selfishness. The purpose of war is not for the loot of the private soldier, neither is the purpose of marriage for the loot of life. Like Apostles husband and wife have been sent out two by two, not that they might only eat and drink, buy and sell, but that they might enrich the Kingdom of God with life and love and not with death.

The soil that takes the seed in the springtime is not unfaithful to its messiahship of harvest, so neither may husband and wife play recreant to the responsibilities of love. The fires of heaven which have been handed down to them as an altar have not been given for their own burning, but that they may pass on the torch that other fires may climb back into the heavens from which they came.

Marital love is happiest when it becomes an earthly Trinity: father, mother and offspring, for by filling up the lacking measure of each in the store of the other, there is built up that natural complement wherein their love is immortalized in the offspring. If love were merely a quest or a romance, it would be incomplete; on the other hand, if it were only a capture and an attainment, it would cease to rise. Only in heaven can there be combined perfectly the joy of the chase and the thrill of the capture, for once having attained God, we will have captured something so Infinitely Beautiful it will take an eternity of chase to sound the depths. But here on earth, God has given to those who are faithful in the Sacrament, a dim sharing in those joys, wherein two hearts in their capture conspire against their mutual impotence and recover the thrill of chase in following their young down the roads that lead to the Kingdom of God. It was a family in the beginning that drew a world of Wise Men and Shepherds, Jews and Gentiles to the

Secret of Eternal Peace. It will be through the family too that America will be reborn. When the day comes when mothers will consider it their greatest glory to be the sacristans of love's fruit, and when fathers will regard it their noblest achievement to be stewards of love's anointed ones, and when children realize that nature sets no limit on the number of uncles one might have, but that a man can have one mother—then America will be great with the greatness of its Founding Fathers and the greatness of a nation blessed by God.

CHAPTER SEVEN

Democracy in Education

Just as Christian principles demand that democracy be extended economically so as to give both capital and labour a share in the profits, management and ownership of industry; and that democracy be extended politically by a recognition of those naturally formed associations in social and economic life, so too, the Christian order demands education be made more democratic, by widening its influence so that it satisfies not only the atheist, but also the believer. At the present time the only group education really caters to is the group that neither practices nor believes in any religion.

Once upon a time religion was considered indispensable to learning; now learning dispenses with religion. Once man had to know why he was living in order that he might know how to live; now he is told how to live without ever knowing why.

We are in a condition of society where the school has replaced the Church in education, and we are coming to a condition where the State will replace the school. Such is always the logic of history; when the family surrenders its rights, the State assumes them as its own. In order to avoid that condition, the new order must integrate in some way religion to education.

Mr. Walter Lippmann, addressing the American Association for the Advancement of Science on December 29, 1940, stated: "The prevailing education is destined, if it continues, to destroy the Western civilization, and in fact, is destroying it. . . . The plain fact is that the graduates of the modern school are actors in the catastrophe which has befallen our civilization. . . . Modern education is based on a denial that it is necessary, or useful, or desirable for the schools and colleges to continue to transmit from generation to generation, the religious, and classical culture of the Western World. . . . By separating education from the classical, religious tradition the school cannot train the pupil to look upon himself as an inviolable person because he is made in the image of God. These very words, though they now sound archaic, are the noblest words in our language." And more lately still on July 4, 1942, he wrote: "In the American schools and colleges, we have gone very far towards abandoning the idea that an education should be grounded upon the deliberate training of the mind and upon a discipline in the making of moral choices. . . . So when this war is over, we have a rendezvous with ourselves to consider as a matter of high priority, the restoration and the reconstruction of American education."

President Hutchins of the University of Chicago, in June 1940, said: "In order to believe in democracy we must believe that there is a difference between truth and falsity, good and bad, right and wrong, and that truth, goodness and right are objective (not subjective) standards, even though they cannot be verified experimentally. . . . Are we prepared to defend these principles? Of course we are not. For forty years and more our intellectual readers have been telling us that they are not true. . . . In the whole realm of social thought there can be nothing but opinion. Since there is nothing but opinion, everybody is entitled to his own opinion. . . . If everything is a matter of opinion, force becomes the only way of settling differences of opinion. And of course, if success is the test of rightness, right is on the side of the heavier battalions."

Our great country was founded on the principle of the separation of Church and the State, and we have no desire to change this principle; but our country was not founded on the principle of the separation of religion and the State.

It was intended that no particular religion should be the national religion, but it was never intended that the nation should be devoid of religion. This is evident both from the words of great Americans and from the tradition of our government.

As George Washington said: "Of all the dispositions and habits which lead to political prosperity, religion and morality are indispensable supports. In vain would that man claim the tribute of patriotism who should labour to subvert these great pillars of human happiness. . . . We ought to be no less persuaded that the propitious smiles of heaven can never be expected on a nation that disregards the eternal rules of order and right which heaven itself has ordained."

The United States Supreme Court, on February 29, 1892, after an elaborate review of legal decisions, laws, and constitutional history declared: "The reasons presented affirm and reaffirm that this is a religious nation. . . ."

And Abraham Lincoln once said: "It is the duty of nations as well as of men to own their dependence upon the overruling power of God; to confess their sins and transgressions in humble sorrow, yet with the assured hope that genuine repentance will lead to mercy and pardon; and to recognize the sublime truth announced in the Holy Scriptures and proven by all history, that these nations alone are blessed."

The First Amendment to the constitution forbids the establishment of any religion as a national religion; this was because there was an established religion in eight of the thirteen colonies—Congregationalism in three; Episcopalianism in five. Furthermore, the same amendment ordered that Congress shall make no laws prohibiting the free exercise of religion. It did not, as for example, Article 124 of the Soviet Constitution, reserve the right to the State to propagandize for atheism and deny it to religion.

Similar provisions for religion are found in the State Constitutions, most of which legislate against a union of the Church and the State, but none of which legislate against the union of religion and the State, as their distinction between the word "sectarian" and "religion" proves. That attitude of the Founding Fathers is well expressed in the Ordinance of 1787 providing for the development of the Northwest, which Ordinance clearly associated religion with education: "Religion, morality and knowledge being necessary to good government and the happiness of mankind, schools and the means of education shall be forever encouraged."

Coming up to the present, The White House Conference of 1940 stated: "The child needs to have a personal appreciation of ethical values consistent with a developing philosophy of life. . . . Here the potent influence of religion can give to the child a conviction of the intrinsic worth of persons and also assurance that he has a significant and secure place in an ordered universe."

President Roosevelt has said: "We are concerned about the children who are outside the reach of religious influences and are denied help in attaining faith in an ordered universe and in the Fatherhood of God. . . . Practical steps should be taken to make more available to children and youth through education the resources of religion as an important factor in the democratic way of life and in the development of personal and social integrity."

It was assumed in American tradition that education would be moral and religious. It was left to the freedom of the religious groups to undertake education. The State would favour no particular religion, but it would welcome any religion. For that reason all the early colleges of the United States were founded with a distinctly religious basis: Harvard, Yale, Princeton, Columbia, Pennsylvania, Brown, Rutgers and Dartmouth. Harvard was founded in 1636 to save Churches from an illiterate ministry. William and Mary was founded in 1693 for the same purpose. Yale in 1701 declared its aim was to prepare young men for "public employment both in Church and Civil State." Columbia was established in 1753 with the chief objective "to teach and engage children to know God in Jesus Christ." Of the 119 colleges founded east of the Mississippi, 104 were Christian and all of them were primarily for Christian purposes. Of 246 founded by 1860, only 17 were State Universities. The Academy, the precursor of our modern high school which had its rise about 1750, and its highest development in 1850, was definitely religious in character.

Very few of these early colleges and universities have retained religion as an integral part of education. An investigation made some years ago recalled that some colleges had reduced the number of students believing in God from one in five at entrance, to one in twenty at graduation.

Dr. Alexander Meiklejohn blames the decline of religion in these institutions on the Churches which have surrendered their fundamental beliefs. "For the most part the revolutionary transfer of power from the Church to the State has happened with the consent, and even on the initiative, of the Churches themselves. Slowly, it is true, especially in England and reluctantly in many other cases, these Churches have deprived themselves of one of their most cherished prerogatives. We Protestants have torn our teaching up loose from its roots, we have broken its connection with the religious beliefs out of which it has grown."

But while these great institutions which once were religious have now become secular, one cannot point to a single Catholic college or university founded by Catholics one hundred, or one hundred and fifty, years ago which is not now as Catholic as ever.

Congregationalists had 700 Churches ministering to the needs of the early American youth at the time of the American Revolution; Baptists had 421; Lutherans had 60; Dutch Reformed had 82 and the Catholics had 52. In each and every instance, religion and education were synonymous to these groups. Certainly no one will deny that the Catholic Church has consistently kept education and religion together. The Catholic Church today has 10,459 schools, 83,515 religious teachers, and 2,584,461 students, all supported by Catholics themselves.

In other words, only the Catholic colleges and universities and other Church colleges are in the spirit and tradition of the Founding Fathers. We have kept the Faith with America. And we are not saying this boastfully, but regretfully. A great burden has been placed on us which we cannot bear. The other Churches were supposed to help carry this burden of preserving the religious and the moral foundations of the country. They have shirked the burden. Today we are left practically alone.

John Erskine after saying that "where morality—that is, personal obligation and responsibility—is not taught from the home up, the educational system first becomes an expensive folly, then an organized racket." He goes on to say: "Before I attempt to make good this charge, I must note two exceptions. The military schools, particularly the academies at West Point and Annapolis, teach responsibility and train character. . . . The other exception which in justice should be named, is the Roman Catholic Schools. They too inculcate a system of personal ethics; they too educate their students in matter of character."

Are we not complaining against the Nazis today because they will not allow the Jew, the Protestants and the Catholics their freedom to educate their youth? Yet under the present system a religious education by Jew, Protestant or Catholic cannot be given except under the prohibitive system of building their own schools.

Education as it is presently constituted is not the bulwark of the nation. Washington said that it should be; but it is not. And the reason is because the college, in taking over the function of the Church, failed to supply a body of beliefs which could sustain the nation in time of trouble. Religion has a social function; that is, to give citizens a set of principles, a hierarchy of value, fundamental convictions and beliefs, and a set of moral standards.

We need these standards and beliefs today, but who shall say what are the beliefs of an educational system? There is no agreement on principles and no uniform set of values. In time of peace the only universal agreement was a negative one, namely, that the Church is non-essential; and in time of war, another negative one, a hatred of Hitler.

Education now affirms that the function which was once performed by religion can be better performed by a school without religion.

The result is that in time of a crisis such as this, we lack a positive belief and a unifying inspiration of sacrifice. As Calvin Coolidge said in May 1928, "Unless our people are thoroughly instructed in the great truths of religion, they are not fitted to understand our institutions, or to provide them with adequate support."

We are at a stage like unto that developed by Dosto-evsky in his *Crime and Punishment*, in which he describes the world as having been desolated by a microbe which affected the intellect and the will rather than the body. The effect of being poisoned by these bacteria was that one imagined there was no law or authority outside himself; that he was the final standard and arbiter of right and wrong; and that all his scientific conclusions and judgments were absolutely right, because they were his.

Whole populations became infected, and no one could understand anyone else; each considered himself as the possessor of the greatest truth; and when someone insisted on his great truth, another would throw his arms in the air and complain about the stupidity of the first. Not only could no one agree with anyone else, but there was no out-side standard by which they could be judged, no moral judgment by which to arbitrate a dispute. The result was that there was only chaos in the world, which ended in a great strife in which every man rose up to kill his brother.

And this picture is fairly accurate. No one in his right mind will admit that universal education has brought us freedom from evil.

One unforeseen stumbling-block has been the in-
evitable impoverishment in the intellectual results
of Education when the process is reduced to its elements and is divorced from its traditional, social
and cultural background in order to make it "available" for "the masses" . . . The possibility of turning
Education to account as a means of amusement for
the masses—and of profit for the entrepreneurs by
whom the amusement is purveyed—has only arisen
since the introduction of Universal Education of
an elementary kind; and this new possibility has
conjured up a third stumbling-block which is the
greatest of all; for it is this that has cheated our ed-
ucationalists, when they have cast their bread upon
the waters, of their expectation of finding it after
many days. The bread of Universal Education is
no sooner cast upon the waters of social life than a
shoal of sharks rises from the depths and devours the
children's bread under the philanthropists' eyes. In
the educational history of England, for example, the
dates speak for themselves. Universal compulsory
gratuitous public instruction was inaugurated in this
country in A.D. 1870; the Yellow Press was invented
some twenty years later—as soon as the first generation of children from the national schools had come
into the labour market and acquired some purchas-
ing power—by a stroke of irresponsible genius which
had divined that the educational philanthropist's
labour of love could be made to yield the newspaper-
king a royal profit.[1]

---

[1] From Arnold J. Toynbee, *A Study of History*, pp. 193, 194 (1935).
Oxford University Press.

Ignorance is not the cause of evil; hence universal education of the intellect alone will not remove evil. It is not the educated who are the good. In fact, the great marvel about St. Thomas is that in being so learned, he was also so very saintly, and not the other way round. What is the use of piling up knowledge, unless we know what we are going to do with it? Facts are for the purpose of feeding values and the moral ends of living; but when our education is devoid of these things, we leave the facts hanging in mid-air. If they are taken into the mind, they remain as so much undigested knowledge which through constipation mars mental and moral judgments. We are all agreed that the young should know something, but there is no agreement as to the one thing everyone ought to know.

Upon what principles shall we proceed?

First, educate the whole man, not the part man. The whole man is not only economic, nor political, nor sexual, but is moral. Because he is moral, he is economic, political, and social, and not vice versa. The education of the whole man entails education on three levels: man must be informed about what takes place on the sub-human level, and thus become acquainted with the Natural Sciences; he must become acquainted with what takes place on the Human Level, and hence know the Humanities and Metaphysics. Finally he must become acquainted with what takes place on the supra-human level, and hence be taught something about God and the moral law and his eternal destiny.

Secondly, as a basic principle of the rights of education, the family, because instituted by God, has a priority of nature and therefore of right over civil society. Existence does not come from the State, hence the parents' rights of education is anterior to a right of civil power and the State.

The State derives its power to educate from the family; the State does not give it to the family.

Third, restore education back again to the Churches and to religion. We are at present in an era of transition in education, and coming into an era wherein education will belong to the family which insists on religion, or to the State which will exclude it. No one wants education to be the unique and fundamental right of the State because such is the essence of Nazism. As H. M. Tomlinson put it in his *All Our Yesterdays*, "My church is down (I hear him saying), my God has been deposed again. There is another God now the State, the State Almighty. I tell you that God will be worse than Moloch. You had better keep that in mind. It has no vision: it has only expediency. It has no morality, only power. And it will have no arts for it will punish the free spirit with death. It will allow no freedom, only uniformity. Its altar will be the ballot-box, and that will be a lie. Right before us is its pillar of fire. It has a heart of gun metal and its belly is full of wheels. You will have to face the brute, you will have to face it. It is nothing but your worst, nothing but the worst of us, lifted up. The children are being fed to it."[2]

Fourth, in a country such as this where there are different religious beliefs, it is the duty of the State to leave free scope to the initiative of the Church and the family while giving them such assistance as justice demands. As we stated before, the pagan element alone in our population is given the benefit of tax money. As Nicholas Murray Butler said: "Even the formal prayer which opens each session of the United States Senate and each session of the House of Representatives, and which accompanies the inauguration

---

[2] Published by Harper & Brothers.

of each president of the United States, would not be permitted in a tax-supported school."

Just how the principle of freedom and equality of all citizens is to be worked out is the business of the State. But the suggestion of the principle is sound Americanism, as President Hutchins has so well said: "The States may, if they choose, assist pupils to attend the schools of their choice. Since we want all American children to get as good an education as they can, since we know that some children will not voluntarily attend public schools, and since we are not prepared to compel them to do so, it is in the public interest to give permission to use Federal grants to help them to go to the schools they will attend and to make these schools as good as possible."

We are at the crossroads of our national history. In the field of education we will either believe or we will obey. He who will not believe in Truth must submit to Power. Which will it be? Will we retain a set of beliefs in which we are all agreed, and on which we were all agreed when this country was founded, or, scrapping all beliefs, will we obey the State which will determine what these beliefs shall be and thus extinguish all freedom?

Let no one who hates religion falsely think that we can do without religion or that it can be banished from the earth. That is the false assumption under which modern pagans work. Nazism has revealed its fallacy better than any argument of mine. The choice is not between religion and no religion, but between two religions; a religion from God or a State religion; a religion with a Cross or religion with a Double Cross.

We do not yet realize this truth, but it is an indisputable fact that a nation's education is far more important than a nation's government. Given one generation educated on the principle that there is no absolute Truth or Justice and our next generation will be a government of Power.

There is no such thing as neutral education; that is, education without morality and religion. Religion and morality are not related to education like raisins to a cake, but as a soul to a body. There can be a cake without raisins, but there cannot be a man without a soul. If education does not inculcate a moral outlook, it will inculcate a materialist or a Communist or a Nazi outlook. Neutrality is absolutely impossible in education. By the mere fact that religious and moral training is neglected, a non-religious, non-morality and by consequence an anti-religious and anti-moral ideology will be developed. "He that is not with me is against me" (Matt. 12: 30).

The old notion of "no indoctrination" really meant "no religion," but instead of "no indoctrination" of faith, it really meant "indoctrination of doubt and unbelief." And doubt is the accomplice of tyranny; if we educate pagans in one generation, we will educate barbarians in the next. As William Penn said: "Men must be governed by God or they will be ruled by tyrants."

The Liberalism of the last century despised all dogmas, not realizing that in divorcing culture from dogmas it asserted a dogma—the false dogma that man has no soul, no supra-temporal purpose, no other goal than to make money, wed and die. In Germany, in Russia, and in Japan, for years education has been built around a creed—either racial, atheistic, or dynastic. To it the young subscribed, they believed in it with enthusiasm. And while we have to go to war against these creeds, our educators at home regard it a waste of time to discuss whether children should be taught to believe in Him Whose love is perfect freedom. The question before us as a nation is not whether religion shall be taught as one subject among many, but whether the integrating principle of all subjects will be derived from the spiritual and Absolute Truth, or from the material and omnipotent State.

The modern world has confused the extension of education with intension, and by spreading it thin has sacrificed its depth. This does not mean that universal education is wrong. No! It is not the universality of it that is wrong, but its lack of a philosophy of life and a proper understanding of the man to be educated. The natural or "neutral" man, as the intelligentsia call him, is antisocial and can be counted on to abuse society for his own personal ends. The only way this egotistic impulse can be combatted is by a renewal of his nature from above. This rebirth alone enables him to be a member of society without losing his personal dignity. There is no disputing the necessity of controlling selfish tendencies. The choice is in whether the State will control it by its omnipotence. The whole of civilized man is to-day confronted with this question: "To whom do you belong?" Education will give the answer.

Neglect conscience, and the majority makes right; neglect the absoluteness of Divine Truths which religion teaches, and you enthrone Power as the only criterion of right and wrong. Neglect the training of Freedom, as liberty within the law, as religion teaches, and you enthrone first a liberty without law which is anarchy, and then by reaction a law without liberty which is Totalitarianism. Neglect the principle that evil is rooted in a perverse will, which religion teaches, and you train the intellect to the neglect of the will and thus end in a system where reason is used to support the passions. Neglect the principle that the progress of man is conditioned upon the progressive diminution of original sin, and you create a fatalistic belief in progress which is unable to stand either the shock of depression or the bloodshed of war. Neglect the ideal that man was made for happiness as religion teaches, and exalt the idea that man was made to make money and you build a race of profiteers, but not a race of Americans.

The hour is past when anyone can say, "I belong to nobody, because I belong to myself." We will belong either to Cæsar or we will belong to God. It was Christianity in the beginning that deprived Cæsar of his unrestricted power over the individuals, and it was through the martyrs' blood that it was accomplished. It is through their blood today, that modern Cæsars are challenged.

That America may be preserved from such a necessity, it must close the gap between the principle of democracy and its education. Our democracy is founded on the principle that our rights come from God: "The Creator has endowed man with certain unalienable rights." Education has a tendency to divorce these human rights from God. It cannot be done. If our rights come from God, no one can take them away—they are "unalienable" as the Declaration of Independence puts it. If they come from the State, the State can take them away.

Certainly, we have rights, but there are never any rights without duties. In fact, duties are opportunities for acquiring rights. Because God made us free; we have rights. Because God made us creatures; we have duties. For over one hundred and fifty years we have been celebrating the ten articles of the Bill of Rights. It is now about time to recall the Ten Commandments in our Bill of Duties!

Here is the dilemma facing this country. On the one hand, government admits that good citizenship is impossible without religion and morality, and that such an integration has been our philosophy of democracy from the beginning.

On the other hand, what encouragement is given by the States to foster religious and moral education? The White House Conference stated that of the thirty million children between the ages of five and seventeen, sixteen million receive no religious education. When you take out of this sixteen million, those who are being educated by the Catholic Church at its expense the number becomes more staggering still.

If this condition existed in less important matters, it would have been remedied long ago. If, for example, it had been discovered that the geography of Russia was left out of our schools, how quickly it would be inserted. Why is nothing done about that which our tradition says is the indispensable condition of democracy? If the government has no scruples about spending millions for boon-doggling, why should it scruple about saving morality and religion?

Any doubts about the importance of religion to resist political slavery can be dissipated by inquiring into the forces which resisted it in our modern crisis. When Hitler came into power in 1933, the first to capitulate were the professors, and the one force which never capitulated was religion, such as the Catholic bishops and Pastor Niemoeller. It was the professors who allowed the independent administration of the universities to be abolished, the universities offering no objections to State elected "Rektoren" and "Dekane" who were forced upon them. It was a bitter disappointment for all who considered the German universities the defender of rights and justice, but when one considers the extremes to which specialization had been carried, and a unified philosophy of life so universally abandoned, there was no one idea around which they could rally.

Given a crisis in any country in the world in which Totalitarianism in any form threatens the liberty of its citizens, the first to capitulate will be the non-religious educators. How could it be otherwise for, without a faith, how could they oppose a faith? It will be only those schools which give a moral and religious training which will challenge the right of the State to dominate the soul of man.

That is why the safeguard of democracy and freedom is in the extension of religious and moral training, and not in its suppression through excessive burdens. There is no reason in the world why any school in the United States which teaches religion and morality should be penalized for being patriotic, or for giving to the nation the two supports without which, as Washington told us, a nation cannot endure.

The prime purpose of education is the making of a man, and it is impossible to make a man without giving him the purpose of being a man. Unless we make sense out of life, we fail in education. Life can be bearable without football, without fraternities, without junior proms, without moving pictures, without a cheap press, without a cocktail hour, but life cannot be bearable unless a coordinating and evaluating principle is given to these and all other activities of life. So long as we educate without defining the purpose of life and the standards of life and without developing a sense of right and wrong, we are losing our souls.

It is up to the country in these days, when an old order is passing, to decide whether we shall allow our soldiers to die for the defence of Christian liberty and justice on the battlefields of the world, and at the same time allow our schools to kill that Christian heritage in the minds of the young. There is something very contradictory about our war cry that we are fighting to preserve a Christian civilization, and a continuance of an education which ignores or destroys it. It is not fair, it is not democratic, it is not American to cater only to the non-religious. A government "of the people, for the people, and by the people" should respect the will of those who believe in religion and morality, even though they be in the minority, for democracy is not the preserver of majority privileges, but the preserver of minority rights.

No signer of the Declaration of Independence was educated in a non-religious school. For a century the United States did not have a single president who was educated in a non-religious school. The only time the State now recognizes religion is when it builds a chapel in a penitentiary. Would it not be a good idea to give a religious training before men get into the penitentiary?

Centuries ago the Light of the World rebuked those whom He called to be teachers, because they ignored little ones: "Suffer the little children and forbid them not to come unto me: for the kingdom of heaven is for such" (Matt. 19: 14). That Master is crying out to them now, Hitler has said: Suffer the little children to come unto me, for of such is the essence of Totalitarianism. There is the dilemma: the children of our country will belong either to God or to the State.

CHAPTER EIGHT

The Need of an Absolute

How to overcome this evil we are fighting against? In order to answer this question one must know the strength of the enemy. In all human forces there are two factors: physical and psychological. The first is the ability to fight; the second is the zeal with which one fights. A weaker weapon in the hand of a man who has a great passion for his cause, will overcome a stronger weapon in the hands of a man who has little or no faith in his cause, or who does not know what he is fighting for.

From a purely material point of view, our enemies are well armed—technically perfect. But their great strength lies in a psychological factor; they believe in an absolute. They have a dogma, a creed, a faith, a religion. Call it a pseudo-mysticism, for that is what it is, but it is still a re-ligion in the sense that it gives the people a faith and a loyalty around which they can rally. That pseudo-religion may be centered about a race, an emperor, a Cæsar, or a corpse, but in its essence it is the same: the affirmation of another absolute than God.

Thanks to it, they have an impetus for action which is wanting to those who are without faith. Not only do they have a passionate devotion to this absolute, but their bodies and their armies are steeled to such a passionate commitment to that faith, that they are willing to sacrifice everything for it, even life itself. Call it fanaticism, call it diabolical, the fact of the matter is that the Nazis are men of faith; they have faith in the primitive purity of their race, faith in the Messianic call to be the masters of the world. From that faith has come those un-Pentecostal fires which in the course of less than ten years swept them into the fury of the strongest army the world has ever seen.

It is no answer to say that their faith is false—certainly it is—it is like the faith of the demons in hell. But without a faith nothing great can ever be accomplished. The faith of the demons inspires them to the ceaseless energy of the destruction of the Kingdom of God, as the faith of the saints inspires them unto its building.

Whence came this fanaticism for an absolute? It is the manifestation in a false form of the zeal which men should have for a true faith. For the last two centuries it has been a fault of the Western World to ridicule zeal for religion. Tolerance which should have been applied to persons was transferred to truths, so that we became indifferent to right and to truth and to error. The zeal which men should have for the true God, could not long be kept chilled and frozen by indifference and our so-called broad-mindedness; it finally swept up through the surface and came out as fanaticism for false gods. The young people in these totalitarian countries were dissatisfied with the husks of a securalized culture; they wanted an absolute that would command conviction, the hardy wine of sacrifice, a truth for souls and a fire for hearts, and an altar for oblations, and they found it in a religion which is anti-religion. Their answer to a civilization that had forgotten the Christian religion was to be anti-Christian, to erect a counter-Church of the City of Man which would war against the City of God until the end of time. That is why the world today is in the peculiar mood of having more energy for the spread of the false gods of race and class and power than it has for the spread of knowledge of the true God of Life and of Love.

The human heart must have an absolute. As Voltaire has said: "If man had no God, he would make a God for himself." Deny man the right to make a pilgrimage to the shrine of a saint, and in fifty years he will be making pilgrimages to a tank factory. Deny man a God Incarnate, and in a few generations he will adore the emperor as the incarnation of a sun god; deny man the right to worship one who rose from a tomb, and in a decade he will try to immortalize a corpse. The totalitarian powers have convinced us that man cannot live without a religion, a faith and an absolute. The question no longer is whether we will or will not have an absolute; the only question is which absolute will we have?

This very enthusiasm for false gods is the explanation of their cruelty. There is nothing temporal that can bear the strain of being deified; it is like placing a marble bust on the stem of a rose; it distorts man like beating a cripple with his own crutches. Endow a machine with infinite power and it will kill you; endow a finite human being with the power of an infinite God, and he will slay you. "Absolute power," as Lord Acton says, "corrupts absolutely." And as Chesterton said, speaking of the horrors of the new religion: "God is more good to the gods that mocked Him, than men are good to the gods they made."

When therefore a man with an eternal destiny is enlisted in the service of our earthly absolute, he becomes its fiercest and its most fanatical soldier. And therein is the totalitarian strength—it is a religion—the animal religion of false gods to whom its devotees pray, in the language of Lady Macbeth:

> Come you spirits . . . And fill me from the crown to toe, top-full of direst cruelty! Make thick my blood: stop up the access and passage to remorse, that no compunctious visitings of nature shake my fell purpose, nor keep peace between the effect and it.[1]

Our problem is how to overcome that false absolute.

Not by hate. There is a group in our midst who, feeling the lack of a great crusading idea and sensing the need of zest in battle, offer the substitute of hate. They contend that the condition of victory is a hatred of the enemies. Hatred is a poor alternative for faith; it inspires men to fight more because their enemy is wicked, rather than because their cause is righteous. It looks to the poison of their own arrows, rather than the justice of their targets. Lamenting the wickedness of our enemies will make us cruel; but it will never make us strong. I would rather think that our soldiers were inspired more by the country they loved than by a country they hated. If we spend our war time sitting on the eggs of hate, in vain will we expect to hatch the dove of peace. As Milton wrote: "Nor can true reconcilement grow, where wounds of deadly hate have pierced so deep."[2]

---

[1] Shakespeare, *Macbeth*.

[2] *Paradise Lost*, Book IV.

Neither shall this false absolute be overcome by force alone, for no idea can be killed by force. A false idea can be conquered only by a true idea; a false dogma, only by a true dogma. When Hitler says the power of money is dead, we must not counter with a defence of financial plutocracy, but with a new idea in which money shall be exclusively a medium of exchange; when Hitler says the power of monopolistic capitalism is dead, we must not defend its abuses but counter with a new idea of economics based on the moral order.

Neither will we overcome the false absolute by indifference to any absolute, or by saying that we were fighting to preserve the *status quo*. A good simple soul on being asked the meaning of *status quo*, defined it rather correctly as the "mess we are in." We are not fighting to keep the world just as it was; if we were we would be fighting to preserve a world that produced a Hitler and Communism and Fascism. We are not fighting to keep just what we have, otherwise we would be defending our personal or sectional interests rather than the good of all.

No vague sentiments about liberalism; no catchwords about freedom of the press; no great mass production however great the eight-hour sacrifice of those who make it; no American sportsmanship transplanted from a football field to a sea or a fox hole; no boasting and bragging, no complaining or haranguing of our public officials and no change of legislators will carry us safely through this crisis, unless we are prepared to give up our coat in time of fire or our cargo in the case of a sinking ship. The Saviour was right when He spoke of the crisis that faced Jerusalem: "Go not back, for your coat . . . Let it perish."

Their strength is in their absolute; ours is in the want of it. Their force is their ideology; our weakness is the lack of it. They were sweeping ahead because they have sure dogmas; we were falling behind because we have none. The dynamism of a false paganism cannot be overcome by the irreligion of a democracy. The enthusiasm for false gods cannot be drowned by an indifference to the true God. No secularized, non-religious theory of political freedom is strong enough to overcome them. A people who lack the strength of an ultimate conviction, cannot overcome their faith or their false absolute. The effective answer to a false religion is not indifference to all religion, but the practice of a true religion. Their totalitarian, false religion can be overcome only by a total true religion. If they have made a politics into a false religion, we shall have to see that religion has something to say about politics.

Unless there is a positive conviction to pit against the assaults of the demon, the citadel of the soul will fall. In other words, what we need above all things is the OFFENSIVE OF A GREAT IDEA.

Is there place for an absolute in American Democracy? There are those who say that democracy by its nature is relative—indifferent to all ideas as equally valid, and therefore it can have no absolute. This is not true. Democracy is based on a political and economic relative, but on a theological absolute. That is to say, it tolerates all political and economic policies and suggestions which contribute to democracy, but it is intolerant about the foundation of democracy.

If we doubt this we need only read the Declaration of Independence which affirms that the "Creator has endowed man with certain unalienable rights." The state is not autonomous, but subject to a higher law. Power thus becomes responsibility. God is the absolute in democracy.

Democracy will rest on this Divine Foundation, or it will be laid to rest. There are no rights of man without duties to God, and if we doubt it, then point to any totalitarian system which denies the rights of man and I will show you they also deny duties to God. Democracy, the value of a person, liberty and the like, are fruits that grow on the tree of belief in God.

These totalitarian powers have thrown down the challenge to us by reminding us that we cannot preserve the fruits of moral order unless we keep the roots. Trying to preserve freedom and democracy without God, in Whom they are grounded, is like preserving the false teeth of a drowning man. If we save the man, we will save his teeth; and if we save our souls in God, we will save our democracy and freedom, but not otherwise.

We cannot equate democracy with Christianity, but we can see that democracy can grow only the seeds which Christianity planted, and indeed from which it has historically sprung.

The world today is choosing its Absolute. The totalitarian systems have chosen their false gods. The only other alternative is the true God. There are only two ideas in all the world. If men do not adore the true Absolute, they will adore a false one. Hitler and others have gone before the world with a New Order—and that it is; new, not only in its politics and economics, but new in its foundation, its religion, its cruelty, its pragmatism and its force. We cannot conquer that New Order by seeking to preserve an Old Order from which it came. The one and only effective means is to build a New Order ourselves—one grounded on the true absolute of God and on His principles of justice and morality.

Idolatry can be overcome only by worship and to worship is to quicken our conscience by the moral law of God, to enlighten our mind with the truth of God, to strengthen our will with the grace of God, and to open our heart to love of God, and to dedicate our purposes to the sovereign will of God. Only a faith can prevail against a faith.

CHAPTER NINE

The Roots of
Democracy and Peace

The word "crisis" in Greek means judgment. A crisis in history is therefore a "verdict of history" upon the way any given civilization has lived and thought, married and unmarried, bought and sold, prayed and cursed. That we are at such a crisis in history today is a commonplace. That this crisis is due to the progressive repudiation of Christian culture and the moral law is unfortunately not the thought of the "Common Man." It is still too universally believed that a shifting of political and economic forces, or a new banking system, will cure our ills. The heart of the crisis is not in these epiphenomena; it is rather in the abdication of conscience.

We are at the end of an era of history, just as definitely as Rome was at the end of an era when Alaric knocked at its Salarian gates. The difference between that crisis and ours is that in the case of Rome a material civilization was collapsing and a spiritual about to emerge. In the present instance, it is the spiritual which is being submerged and the material which is in the ascendancy.

The story of Western civilization, like the dramas of the Periclean Age, can be divided into three stages. First there was a Christian civilization. Then there followed what might be called the Era of Substitution; in the last four hundred years of the latter era civilization has been trying to find a substitute for the regency of the Moral Law of God in the hearts of individuals and in the councils of nations; among these substitutions were the Divine Right of Kings, the Common Will, Human Reason, the Natural Law understood as Physical Law, and finally individual self-interest. The third and final stage, which is now being ushered in, is probably an era of cyclic wars where the issue will not be between nations but between ideological absolutes. The wars of religion of the sixteenth century have now reached their logical conclusion in the wars of anti-religion.

Our so-called liberal civilization, which is dying, is only a transitional phase between a civilization that once was Christian and one that is anti-Christian. It has no stability of its own, being based for the most part in successive negations of the Christian philosophy of life. It will end either in a return to the Christian tradition or in revulsion against it. This alone constitutes the crisis of democracy; it will either return to its roots or die.

The practical atheism and indifference of the Western World was a preparation for Communism, as Communism is the negative side of Nazism. Liberalism affirms that it makes no difference whether or not you believe in God. Communism answered; it makes a world of difference, because there is no God. Nazism retorted: Communism, you are wrong in saying there is no God. There is a God, but that God is not the God of Justice, he is the God of the German race. Nazism would probably have never come into being had not Communism cleared away the "débris of Christianity," and Communism would never have come into the world if it had not already been "atheized" by millions of individuals. Marx merely socialized individual atheism, turning the atoms of atheism into the molecule of Communistic atheism.

The Western World of the Democracies is therefore partly the cause of this crisis in the sense that it was indifferent to the moral law, but it also provides the remedy in reacting against the terrible evils it has begotten. The spectacle of seeing its retail repudiation of the moral law worked out in a wholesale fashion has scandalized it, and caused it to react. Never before has the cause of democracy been so coincident with Christianity.

We are fighting not to preserve democracy as a particular system or form of government but democracy as a principle, that is, one which recognizes the intrinsic value of man regardless of race, colour, nation or class. More exactly, we are fighting not to preserve democracy but to preserve the roots of democracy.

We are not fighting to preserve the liberal concept of freedom, which understands freedom as the right to do whatever you please; we are not fighting to preserve the Marx-Engels-Hitler concept of freedom as the right to do whatever you must; but rather we are fighting to preserve the Christian concept of freedom, which is the right to do whatever you ought. Freedom from something is meaningless without freedom for something, and that ultimate something is God.

We are not fighting to preserve or create a material equality, which considers men equal when their stomachs are filled with the same brand of caviar or their vaults with the same quantity of bonds. We are fighting to restore a

spiritual equality which denies that any man shall ever
be treated as a means or an instrument, and which affirms that all men are equal because there is a common
denominator outside of men which makes men equal; that
is, God. The Liberal idea of equality was based on free
trade, free money, and equal opportunity to run an economic race; the Christian concept of equality is based on
free men and the equal opportunity of all men to live well,
even though they are too weak, too crippled, or too old,
to enter the economic race. We are fighting for Peace; but
what is Peace? The best definition of Peace the world has
ever had is that given by St. Augustine: "Peace is the tranquillity of order." It is not tranquillity alone, for thieves
dividing their loot, or the corrupt politician enjoying his
spoils may be tranquil. Peace adds to quietude the idea of
"order," which implies a hierarchy or a pyramid in which
each thing is in its proper place and fulfils its proper function. There is order in the bodily organism. The head
and the feet are not equal in dignity, but they are at peace
when each acts according to its nature; their inequality is
of function and therefore involves no injustice. The feet
were made for walking, not for thinking. It would be a
very perverted egalitarianism which would demand that
we be fair to our head and walk on it as much as we do on
our feet.

Since Peace is inseparable from Justice and Charity, it
follows that peace is conditioned upon a moral authority.
This brings us back to the theme that a moral authority is
needed today. This no one will deny. Minds are not universally perverse, but they are confused—they know not what
is right. The criterion of right is agreement with a will or
intention. For example, an engine works well when it con-
forms to the intention which the engineer had in designing

it; a pencil is good when it writes, thus fulfilling the will of its maker.

In like manner, right for man means acting in accordance with the Will of God or the intention God had in creating him. Holiness consists in fixation to that Divine Will. It happens that, since God made man free, man may follow another will than God's Will; for example, his own will, like the prodigal, or the popular will like Pilate. Unfortunately, too many in our day choose the second standard and identify right with the will of the majority, or the mood of the masses, or the spirit of the world.

The millions of the world who keep their fingers on the pulse of public opinion and follow every theory, every vogue, have no standard of right and wrong. A thing cannot measure itself; a tape measure must be outside the cloth; a speedometer must not be a brick in the roadway; a judge must not be a shareholder in the corporation whose cause he judges. In like manner the judgment of the world must be from outside the world. Such a standard is the need of the hour remedy, an authority that does not, like some politician, find out what the people want and then give it to them, but which gives them what is true and good whether it is popular or not. We need someone to be healthy when the world is sick; someone to be a stretcher-bearer when the house is burning; someone to be right when the world is wrong.

A sword can put an end to the war, but it cannot create peace. Peace does not come from the womb of silenced batteries, but from a justice rooted in the Eternal Law of God. As Pius XI said: "To create the atmosphere of lasting peace neither peace treaties nor the most solemn pacts, nor international meetings or conferences, nor even the most disinterested efforts of any statesmen, will be enough, unless in the first place are recognized the sacred rights of natural and divine law."

This moral basis of peace has been to a great extent neglected in the past. Modern wars therefore came less as a surprise to the Church than to the world. For example, when in 1894, Leo XIII warned that the "armed peace which now prevails cannot last much longer," who among the prophets of Progress and Darwin and the brave new world of Huxley believed that that new war would come twenty years almost to the day after the Holy Father foretold it?

When on December 23, 1922, while our optimists were still feeding themselves on Rousseau and the natural goodness of man and boasting that the war of 1914–1918 was a war to end all wars, how many heeded the words of the Holy Father that another world war was near, and that the vengeance of Versailles was devoid of Justice and charity? "Peace," he said, "was indeed signed between the belligerents, not in the hearts of men. The spirit of war still reigns in them, bringing always greater harm to society. Even though arms have been laid down in Europe you know well how the perils of new war are threatening."

For many decades the world has resented the suggestion of an unarmed, responsible, supranational moral force as custodian of a fixed concept of justice. When the Hague Conference was held in 1889, there was a suggestion made that the Holy See be represented as a moral authority. Only one representative of the nations there present favoured the inclusion; and that was the Queen of the Netherlands. In 1907 there was a similar exclusion of the spiritual authority of the Church.

Then came the World War and on April 26, 1915, the Secret Treaty of London was signed, Article 15, of which reads: "France, Great Britain and Russia shall support such opposition as Italy may make to any proposal in the direction of introducing representatives of the Holy See in any peace negotiations or regulations for the Settlement of questions raised by the present war." Article 16: "The present arrangement shall be held secret."

At the close of World War the Treaty of Versailles was signed, but its preamble was unlike all others, for by this time not only men but nations had apostatized from God. Every other treaty involving all the nations Europe had begun as the last such treaty—the treaty of Vienna in 1815—had begun: "In the name of the most Holy and Undivided Trinity." But this new one signaling the advent of a world made safe for democracy, but not Divinity, began "In the name of the High Contracting Parties!"

When Benedict XV published his peace proposals during the last war, Ambassador Jusserand of France called on President Wilson and commented on the excellence of the proposals, to which the President retorted with all humour—I am quoting verbatim: "Why does he want to butt in?"

But all that is in the past. What is the attitude of much of the world today in the midst of war? Note the change! For the past fifty years the world said: "We want no spiritual authority," but for the past two years it asks: "Why does not your spiritual authority have more authority?" The world spent one hundred and fifty years exiling a spiritual force from international relations, and now is angry because that same spiritual force has not kept peace in the house from which it was exiled. The very ones who some twenty years ago did all they could to make the Church weak, now bemoan because it is not strong. The world drove away the shepherd and his sheep and then complained it had no wool. It broke the signposts of peace which the Church erected and blamed the Church because the world lost the way.

What does the Christian spirit suggest to peacemakers? There should be an interval between the cessation of wars and the drawing up of a peace treaty. The ending of the war is distinct from making a durable foundation of peace. The first is to be dictated by the victors; the second is arrived at by consultation with the vanquished. The mistake made in the last war was to identify the two by drawing up the Final Treaty at the beginning. It allowed passions no time to cool, and gave no time to collect facts. As the Holy Father stated in his first Encyclical: "At the end of this war there will be fresh pacts, fresh arrangements of international relations. Will they be conceived in a spirit of justice and fairness all round, in a spirit of reconstruction and peace, or will they disastrously repeat our old and our recent errors? Experience shows it is but an empty dream to expect a real settlement to emerge at the moment when the conflagration of war had died down . . ."

Nations must abandon the idea of their absolute sovereignty in order to give some sovereignty to the international order. The reason no penalties could be imposed on Japan in the case of Manchuria, and on Italy in the case of Abyssinia, was because the problem of sanctions was left to the sovereign States, thus depriving the League of sovereignty. No State wishes to use force even when it should, lest its own vital interests be affected. The common good of the world is not one of the vital interests of any individual nation. Article 13 of the League stated that in the case of disputes, the members would submit the matter to the League if "they recognized it to be suitable." In other words utility and not morality was the basis of whether or not a dispute should be adjudicated. In order to have international sovereignty there must be recognized an authority above the nations. You cannot pack up a suitcase if you go into it, and you cannot bind nations into a unity, unless there is a law and authority outside the nations. The problem of sovereignty thus gets down to something as basic as this: we will either obey one another's politicians, which will never be (for if we do not obey our own, why should we obey someone else's?), or we will recognize a supranational authority or the moral law of God.

Membership in the new international body should be based upon the acceptance of certain basic moral principles, such as the five enunciated in the Papal Program. Practically anyone could enter into the last League. "Any fully self-governing State, Dominion or Colony," the Constitution stated, "may become a member of the League if its admission is agreed to by two thirds of the Assembly." There was no criterion for admission, no required acceptance of common values; Russia with its atheism, Germany with its Nazism, Japan with its Imperialism were all free to enter so long as they received sufficient votes. The only one who protested against Communistic representation in the League was De Valera. The result was that the League was a mechanical structure; it had no organic unity. No wonder it called itself "The High Contracting Parties." It was certainly not an organization of a common civilization and a common faith, sharing a common culture. It was only an artificial piecing together of mosaic-nations on the theory that the State is only the result of a contract.

The new League, or whatever it is to be called, should have higher rates of subscription and admit only those who accept the moral conditions necessary for international peace and justice. Regardless therefore of how much Russia may aid the Allies, if at the close of this war it still insists on denying one of the four freedoms, namely religion, then it should not be admitted to the League. If it does fulfil the condition and grant freedom, then other things being equal, it should be admitted. In other words, the next world peace will not start with ALL the victorious nations, assuming that we win: it will start with the Nations who believe in a moral order. There will be a moral subscription for admittance and not a numerical one.

The Christian spirit demands that this war shall not become the occasion for the expansion of imperialism, regardless of who is interested in doing so. As a result of the last war, Great Britain increased its Empire by 1,607,053 square miles with 35,000,000 inhabitants; the Belgian Empire got 53,000 square miles with 3,387,000 inhabitants. Italy got none and America wanted none. It is very interesting that the difference between Point No. 1 of the Papal Plan for Peace and Article 4 of the Atlantic Charter is that the Holy Father grants "to all nations great or small, powerful or weak, right to life and independence." Article 4 of the Atlantic Charter conditions this upon "existing obligations." His Holiness says that no obligations shall stand in the way of their freedom and independence; the Atlantic Charter says that "present obligations" do so. Therein is the difference between morality and balance of power politics.

In order to bring home the importance of the moral basis for peace, we ask these questions: Why should any of the treaties or pacts signed at the close of this War be kept? What guarantee have we that they will be honoured more at the close of this War than they were at the close of the last? Some lawyers say that treaties should be kept because nations freely enter into them. But what is to prevent the same nations from freely walking out on the treaties, as Russia and Germany did in the case of Poland, Italy in the case of Ethiopia, and Japan in the case of China? Another group holds that treaties are binding because it is advantageous to have them so. Then logic would suggest that as soon as they cease to be advantageous, they are no longer binding.

Another school of jurists argues that treaties should be kept because it is a custom. But does not modern history prove that it is more customary to break treaties than to keep them?

When one gets down to rock bottom, there are only two possible reasons for keeping treaties: either because of force or because of moral obligation. If force, then might makes right. If moral obligation, then the recognition of the natural law and a set of moral principles is superior to the sovereignty of any nation, existing before any nation began, and binding every nation even when its application goes against it. Perhaps it was a deep consciousness of this need that prompted President Roosevelt to say: "We are especially conscious of the Divine Power. It is seeming that at a time like this, we should pray to Almighty God for His blessing on our country and for the establishment of a just and permanent peace among the nations of the world."

CHAPTER TEN

On Whose Side Are We?

Just suppose a sophomore was on his way home from an afternoon class convinced of the idea that there is no distinction between right and wrong. He would then be anti-Christian by conviction. Now suppose that he sees an innocent person assaulted, and immediately springs to his defence. He would thus disprove by practice what he believed in theory. He would be on the side of absolute goodness through force of circumstances. We were like that student. Many Americans believed there was no distinction between right and wrong; thousands believed with Karl Marx, that man had no soul, and therefore democracy was wrong and Communism was right; tens of thousands believed that since there was no Absolute Truth, power was the determinant of truth. But suddenly when other nations began to put these ideas into practice, we became horrified; we were not shocked at their being retailed in America, but when our enemies began to hand them out in wholesale fashion we were shocked beyond expression. We had no idea that the philosophy of expediency was so wrong when a professor in a cap and gown taught it from a rostrum, but we began to realize how awfully wrong it was when a Jap practiced it from an aeroplane over Pearl Harbour. We began to see the fruits of godlessness in the persecution of Jews and Christians, in the denial of basic rights and freedoms, and in the glorification of power over truth.

Like a boy who, given to petty thievery, will sometimes be shocked back into honesty at the sight of a burglar going to jail for life, so America reacted. In the face of expediency and power, we said: "this thing cannot go on; it is too evil; too wicked, too cruel, too inhuman!" We arose to slay the beast. We are fighting for humanity. And since the cause of man is the cause of God, in battling against the dragon of evil, we found ourselves by force of circumstances on the side of God, of man and the God-man Christ. In this sense we are on the Christian side!

Only a small percentage of Americans ever worship God on Sunday; one out of every six marriages end in divorce, despite God's law: "What God hath joined together let no man put asunder"; too many have failed to teach their children to pray and to instill in their hearts the foundation of the virtues of purity and piety. Yes, we have broken God's law a million times and we shall have to do penance. But we have not, like our enemies, identified God with our wicked deeds, or enthroned a corpse as a substitute for the Living God, or made right synonymous with a race or a class or a nation. Our sins leave the way open for penance, amendment, redemption and resurrection. God can use us through amendment as instruments for the restoration of His Justice and Goodness in the world. We have a greater potentiality for Divine Action than our enemies; He can lift us up because, though doing evil, we still believed in a Righteousness above our heads. He can lay His absolving hand upon us as Magdalenes at His feet; we can rise to proclaim the sweetness of the "passionless passion and wild tranquillity" which is the love of God. As He took the bruised and rotted tree of Eden and transformed it into Calvary's tree of Life; as He took the darkened intellect and weak will of an Adam and elevated it to the New man of Nazareth; as He took the proud Eve and made her the instrument of the human race for begetting through His grace the New Eve of the Glorious Virgin Mary, so He in His mercy can use us as His instruments, if we but respond to his love, for the restoration to a world order where shepherds need not be killed because they kneel at a crib, nor Johns be beheaded because they say divorce is wrong. In the sense that the weak, and the blind, and deaf left the way open to His healing power, we too are on God's side!

Three Scriptural figures represent our present position and our hope. Like St. Paul we should say that we are not deserving to be called an apostle; for in our ignorance and like him we opposed the Divine. Our hands are not clean. But that will not prevent us, despite our unworthiness, from becoming good apostles, defending God's cause amidst opposition, putting on the armour of faith and the shield of salvation, so that in the end we may rejoice and say "we laboured more abundantly" than those who never fell away.

We too are like Peter. We denied our faith; we warmed ourselves by the fires of our complacency, we even cursed and swore that we knew not the Christ. But we never abandoned Him, nor set up a false god, nor in our sin, like Judas, despaired of His Mercy and Forgiveness. Rather, like Peter, despite our denials, when the test came and we were forced

to take sides even in the face of death, we were found willing to die for the principles we had once rejected.

But better still, we are like Simon of Cyrene. As his
name implies, he was not a native of Jerusalem. But like
all mankind he was curious at the death of his fellow-
man. So he stationed himself by a Jerusalem roadside to
watch what to him were three common criminals dragging
their gibbets of death to the hill of the skull. He was perfectly indifferent about the whole spectacle:—he was what
we today call "broad-minded." He saw no great issues involved; right and wrong was to him a question of a point
of view. If anyone had told him that he was witnessing the
greatest act of evil of all time—the crucifixion of Truth, and
that from the exhaustion of evil by that deed, life and goodness would come, he would probably have sneered as Pilate
did: "What is Truth?"

But as he stood there an indifferent watcher of the
great drama of redemption, the long arm of Roman Law
reached out in the first military conscription of the Christian ages and laid itself upon his shoulders saying: "Carry
that man's Cross." "Take it up." He did not want to do it;
he had taken no sides. But he was forced to do it. In the
strong language of Sacred Scripture he was "constrained."

Following in the footsteps of the Master with that queer
yoke of the Cross upon him, he made a great discovery. He
began to see that the yoke was sweet, the burden light. His
two sons, Alexandrinus and Rufinus became bishops and
martyrs of the early Church.

That is America! Like Simon we stood as indifferent
spectators on the roadway of our modern Golgotha. We
saw the phenomenon of Totalitarianism arise, with its
anti-Semitism, its "religion is the opium of the people,"
its anti-Christianity, its repudiation of the Sermon on the

Mount. But we at first sight felt we should be broad-minded about these things.

Then suddenly the invasion of Poland, the destruction of the Low Countries, the expulsion of the Jews and Christians, persecution, and the bombing of Pearl Harbour, startled us out of indifference—almost in so many words we were told: "Take up your Cross!" Carry the Cross of Justice, Freedom and Truth and Law that are rooted in God. We did not want that cross of war. We did not ask for it. It was forced on us. But we took it. And like Simon we are trudging along the highway of the centuries carrying something whose meaning is not yet clear. We do not know who gave it to us; we do not yet know all of its meaning; we do not yet know we are carrying the Cross of Christ. That is America today.

This is the issue involved in this war, that is, the choice of absolutes. No one in the United States has put it as clearly as a recent Nazi book published in Berlin entitled: *God and Race: A Soldier's Creed*, by Theodor Frisch, in Chapter II of which we read: "Where there is a struggle there is a front. The fronts are evident; one is called Christ, the other Germany. There is no third front, nor is there any compromise, only one clear decision. Today it is not a question of weakening Catholicism in order to reinforce Protestantism. Today every alien religion is replaced by a flame in the deepest depth of the German soul. Each epoch has its symbol. Two epochs and two symbols are now facing each other; the cross and the sword. Today Christianity is under the sign of the Cross; Christianity, but not the Christian. Our struggle is not against man. It is against an idea. The front of the cross has a strong wing and a weak one. The strong one is Catholicism, the weak one Protestantism. We struggle against both, and the object of the struggle is

Germany. There will be neither dogma nor church, only the German community. No confession, not even a general Christian Church, but only one people that believes in God and itself!"

That is one of the clearest expressions that has yet come from any nation in this World War. Truly indeed, it is a struggle of the cross and the sword. We are on the side of the Cross, Hitler is on the side of the sword. May a day come when, as he reaches out his sword to us, we will be strong enough in virtue of recovery of the Divine Absolute, to seize the naked blade with our bare hands, pull it away from him and lift the sword high in the air with the hilt above and watch the hilt frame against the august blue of heaven's sky the glorious symbol of the Cross of Christ!

Prayer to Obtain a Favor Through the Intercession of Venerable Fulton J. Sheen

———

Eternal Father, You alone grant us
every blessing in Heaven and on earth,
through the redemptive mission of Your
Divine Son, Jesus Christ, and by the
working of the Holy Spirit.
If it be according to Your Will, glorify
Your servant, Archbishop Fulton J.
Sheen, by granting the favor I now request
through his prayerful intercession
(*mention your request*).
I make this prayer confidently through
Jesus Christ, our Lord. Amen.

Imprimatur +Most Rev. Daniel R. Jenky, C.S.C.,
Bishop of Peoria

For information on membership in the Archbishop Fulton J. Sheen Foundation, or to share any personal knowledge of the archbishop (letters, photos, life experiences), or to report any spiritual or physical favors in his name, please write:

The Archbishop Sheen Foundation
P.O. Box 728
Peoria, IL 61652-0728